THE
BAIT STORE

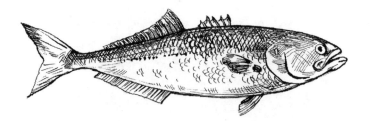

THE

BAIT STORE

& OTHER STORIES

BY RON FURST

ILLUSTRATED BY
ROBERT DOHAR

2016
Great Life Press
Rye, New Hampshire

ISBN: 978-1-938394-19-5
Library of Congress Control Number: 2015949004

Published by:
Great Life Press
Rye, New Hampshire 03870
www.greatlifepress.com

Cover illustration: Chris Holmes

All other illustrations: Robert Dohar

Additional books are available from:
email: info@camphawthorne.org

The stories in this book are based on the author's personal experiences. Some names have been changed.

To the many campers and staff
who generously shared their joy
and energy with my wife and
me during our twenty-four years
together at
Camp Hawthorne

Contents

Preface

I believe that one of life's greatest privileges is to be able to support your loved ones by working in a career that you truly love. Now that I am retired from an active role in the camping industry, I have had more than adequate time to look back at how I managed to create a business that was so much fun.

Our lives are made up of stories. We all have them; some are more interesting than others, but they define our lives, and each brings us the gift of a lesson if we are able to see it. My stories have given me great gifts; indeed, the greatest has been to understand that I haven't managed alone. Once I had a clear mental picture of where I wanted to go in my life, a helpful hand was often extended at crucial moments. Help came from material and nonmaterial realms guiding me toward certain situations that proved useful to me. This intuitive help, I believe, is offered to all from the deeper recesses of our minds, if only we are open to it. Once I learned to trust my inner guidance, I knew the result of my promptings would lead me where I needed to go.

Now I am entering a part of my life best described by Hindu philosophy, which divides human life into four stages. Having passed through my first two stages as a student and householder, I look forward to stepping aside from my public persona and spending more quiet times at my Maine cabin in the mountains, tending my field of potatoes, meditating, and contemplating. My hope is that I can be of service to others in a more advisory capacity, and that these stories of my life will bring a lightness to your heart and be an inspiration to your soul.

The Bait Store

ew young students attending business school would dream of owning a bait store. Let's face it, what doesn't smell bad in a bait store? Who wants to date a man who spends his day hand-counting sea worms, clam necks, mackerel, squid, and live green crabs and placing them into little white boxes to sell? No matter how often you wash your hands, you always take a little bit of the day's work home with you under your fingernails. The only profession less attractive to a young woman might belong to the guy who comes to your home to pump out your septic system. No one should seriously consider owning a bait store unless they are single or part of a rock-solid marriage that could survive the pressures of this volatile business.

So why did I choose to start my first business as a bait store owner while attending business school? To begin with, I never saw myself as someone who would be happy working for other people. I knew deep down in my Jewish roots that someday I would need to strike out on my own to find meaningful employment. It was not that I believed I was smarter or more clever than anyone else; I just felt a need to trust my own instincts and intuition. I did know that to be happy, one needs to find a career to love. And at that time I had a true love that would make me shiver with excitement whenever I thought about it: I loved to fish.

My grandparents owned a cottage on a beach that lined the Cape Cod Canal. From May to October, the swift current of the canal became a highway for both bottom and game fish. Nothing made me happier as a child than being at the Cape house during that time of year. Early each morning when the tide was right, I ran the fifty or so feet from the porch steps of the house to the water's edge carrying my nine-foot fishing rod, a tackle box, and a pint-sized box of sea worms. I loved making believe that it was my job to catch fish to save my family from certain starvation.

As soon as I secured my favorite fishing spot on the beach, my brother Jeffrey, two years my senior, would appear. I would try to persuade him to find his own area to fish, preferably as far away from me as possible. My brother had little patience for fishing and would get his fishing line tangled up with mine and anyone else's within fifty feet of him. More time was spent untangling our lines than actually fishing due to his poor casting skills and the fickle personality of our Penn Squidder bait-casting reels. To make matters worse, he enjoyed sneaking up on me and slipping small live fish down my pants or bathing suit. He preferred perch or dogfish due to their spiny fins. My reaction to his prank was always the same: once I stripped down to nothing and dislodged the fish from my underpants, I searched the beach for the perfect rock impregnated with sharp barnacles and chased him up the hill into the house, aiming straight for his head.

My grandparents were always eager to take us with them to spend part of the summer at the Cape house. Grandpa had a large and gregarious personality and loved having people around. As the former owner of a successful speakeasy in Boston during Prohibition and subsequent nightclubs and restaurants, my grandfather worked his connections and became an important political operative in Boston. Their summer house was a gathering place for Boston politicians, law enforcement commissioners, civic leaders, and parish priests. Grandpa was the person who connected everyone. With a constant stream of guests dropping by for some political favor or advice, the dinner table rarely had fewer than twelve guests.

To feed this multitude, my grandmother needed, among other things, a constant supply of fresh fish. She was like a peasant woman when it came to making good use of the fruits of the sea. Any fish my brother and I were able to catch, even if it was small or bony, would be promptly cleaned and prepared for eating. Flounder, fluke, bass, and codfish were fried up to delight our diners. Tautog, perch, and dogfish were cleaned and used for chowders and fish cakes. Whenever I caught what I thought was a monster of a fish, I would run straight into the house with my fishing rod, dragging the fish behind me still hooked to the line. Grandma always made me feel like I was saving the day; now we would have something special to serve the guests for dinner that evening.

Beginning at age six, I was sent away with my three siblings to overnight camp each summer for eight full weeks. It was my good fortune that our parents found a camp whose directors became my inspiration for many years. I was having a terrible experience in public school due to some learning difficulties. Summer camp became my refuge and a place where I could express my love for nature, sports, and community. I spent many wonderful summers there.

Unfortunately, once I entered college, my father, who owned a paintbrush manufacturing factory, had other plans and insisted it was time for me to learn the family business by spending summers in the factory. I was torn between following my personal dreams and helping my father. After spending so many summers at camp in the Maine woods on a pristine lake, my adjustment to working in a smelly, inner-city factory quickly took its toll. I was suffocating—spiritually and emotionally. Commuting to work through the city traffic just added to my misery.

During my second summer at the factory, I knew I had to leave the business. I had come up with the idea of how much fun it could be to own a bait store on the Cape and thought this an appropriate time to share my idea with two of my dad's best foremen, Clint Hall and Frank McCann, who immediately went right to work to choose the perfect name for the bait store. It was decided by overwhelming consensus that I needed to call the store the Master Baiter. Yes, mixing good-natured humor with fresh bait was going to be part of my mission statement.

Clint and Frank were not satisfied with just choosing the store name; they wanted to help with slogans, signage, and promotion. They envisioned a string of sandwich signs along the road announcing my grand opening, scheduled for the following season's Memorial Day weekend. I chose three of their best ideas and promised them due credits (and free bait) for their combined creative genius. The signs agreed upon were (1) "You're in good hands with the Master Baiter"; (2) "If you can't come, call"; and (3) "Come in and drive it on home."

The following spring, after finishing my junior year of college, I headed for the town of Bourne, considered the gateway to Cape Cod, in search of the perfect location for my new business. My grandparents seemed delighted when I approached them with the idea of being their summer guest at the Cape House. When not working at the store, I planned to resume my role as a provider of fresh fish to the family.

My grandfather assured me that he could convince a local business to rent me a sliver of land for a small building for the store. We began our search at Byron's Fish Market. Grandpa and I saw the pairing of a fish market with a bait store to be quite complementary. Byron immediately saw it differently. "Why should I encourage my local customers to buy bait and catch their own fish when they can walk in and buy fish from me?" he snapped.

After pursuing a few more businesses to no avail, Grandpa grew bored and eager for his afternoon martini. Far from ready to give up on my dream, I drove him home and set out on my own, heading farther away from the center of town where the roadside businesses were less commercial and looked sketchy at best. That was where I met a fruit stand owner named Red.

It might be hard for a first-time tourist to Cape Cod to recognize Red's fruit and vegetable stand as a viable business and not just a pile of rotting vegetables scattered by the side of the road. There was no shelving and no awning or refrigeration to protect Red's produce from the baking heat of the summer sun. Red's "fresh" produce was piled up on empty wooden crates. Backup cases remained in the back of his truck, which resembled something the Marines might have captured from German Feldmarschal Rommel during the WWII African campaign. A series of hand-painted signs on cardboard leaned against the crates along the roadside while an old market scale hung freely from a wooden frame made from two-by-fours.

Red was thin, appeared to be in his late forties, and had a head of curly red hair. He greeted me with a big smile as I stepped out of my green VW. This setting would be perfect for my store if I could get Red caught up in my enthusiasm. Red owned land that had almost 2,000 feet of frontage on the side of the road leading into Cape Cod. I would have plenty of room to place my signs alongside his. Set back about a hundred feet from the road was a shed-style building that Red had rented out. The renter, named Betty, was making it into a drive-up sub shop called the Bay Sub.

What could be more perfect than a sub shop, a fruit stand, and a bait store all on the same piece of property? I explained to Red that I planned to purchase a prefabricated building at Grossman's Lumber. Once erected, customers could just drive up in their car or step up to my outside window to purchase bait, tackle, and whatever else I decided to sell. All I needed was a small piece of land on the far roadside end of his property so that customers could easily see my signs and building.

There was no need for serious negotiations. Red liked the idea and we both agreed that $50 a month was fair rent for a little slice of land. Red even offered to help me put the building up and said I could run heavy-duty extension cords through the trees from the back of the sub shop to power my store. A small donation of $15 a month to Betty, the owner of the Bay Sub would be more than enough. I loved how Red, like me, was apparently always looking for ways to save money, even if they were slightly illegal.

With only $800 saved to begin my business, I had to find every imaginable way to use my funds wisely. The prefab shed, bought and delivered, cost just under $300. It was twelve feet long by eight feet wide, just big enough to house three secondhand refrigerators with adequate space for my worms and frozen bait. Simple finish nails pounded into the wall studs were perfect to hang an assortment of hooks, leaders, rigs, and fishing lures that were popular with Cape Cod anglers.

My college girlfriend was in art school and offered to paint a large sign for me before returning home to New Jersey for the summer. The sign would span the roof of the building. There were four bait stores within a few miles of my store, all with well-established clientele.

Overly superstitious by nature, when fishermen found a bait dealer they liked, they stayed with him. Fishermen relied on their bait dealers to be up on the local fishing scene and to advise them on all matters pertaining to fishing—where the fish were biting and what bait was best suited for their catch. Good signage was key to flagging down new bait customers.

A large sign, however, would not be enough. I needed an angle to encourage fishermen to check out my store. I decided to discount the price of a dozen sea worms from the going Cape Cod price of eighty cents a dozen to sixty-nine cents a dozen. My girlfriend painted a near-professional sign announcing that we were a Discount Bait Store. The large block letters painted in black, red, and white looked great at night, especially once I focused blinking lights on the sign.

Memorial Day weekend, the unofficial beginning of summer, was a week away. I was anxious to get my store up and running for the beginning of the fishing season and the return of game fish from their winter feeding grounds. With the help of a few college friends and Red pitching in at decisive moments, the bait shack was soon in place. I was ready to stock my inventory.

I did some research and found a fishing tackle wholesale company called Boston Camping. I was assigned a salesman named Mel, whose office was adjacent to the showroom where I could pick out gear suited for saltwater fishing on Cape Cod. Mel had an obvious drinking problem and periodically took a quick swig of rye whiskey from a flask hidden in his filing cabinet. He enjoyed taking me into the warehouse to offer special deals on rods and reels. Mel would always round off the cost of what he thought I owed and quickly put the cash into his pocket. It was easy to see what he was up to, but what he did with the money was his business, not mine. Since I needed to replenish my inventory of tackle every two to three weeks, I quickly learned that the deals always got better when I showed up late in the afternoon.

A more pressing need, of course, was for sea worms. I had secured the name and phone number of a bait wholesaler from one of the empty boxes I found behind a bait store down the road. The wholesaler agreed to drop by the following Monday morning to go over prices, delivery schedule, and credit requirements. As soon as he got out of his car, I could see by his face that I was about to hear bad news. Evidently the four established bait store owners down the road had gotten together in the meantime and informed the wholesaler that if he sold me any bait or helped me in any way, they would all find a new wholesaler to supply their businesses. I immediately explained to him that it was illegal for them to pressure him not to sell to me and that there were no other bait dealers on Cape Cod, but he would hear none of it. "Sorry, my hands are tied" is all he said as he quickly returned to his car and drove off.

I had not sold as much as one worm and already there was a conspiracy to run me out of business. With little time to waste, my only option was to plead my case directly to the worm diggers who supplied the wholesalers throughout New England. I knew the industry was centered on the tidal rivers of coastal Maine. After many calls to local chambers of commerce in that area, I learned that the biggest supplier was Frank Hammond, whose business was located on the banks of the Sheepscot River in Wiscasset, Maine. Frank employed over fifty unionized worm diggers who worked the day and evening outgoing tides with waders and pitchforks, hand-picking live sea worms from the mud flats of the retreating river.

Frank Hammond turned out to be one hell of a nice guy. He listened carefully to my situation and was upset to hear about the unfair business practices that I faced. Frank agreed to sell me all the bait I needed at a price that was 35 percent cheaper than what the bait wholesaler on the Cape charged. By eliminating the middle man, I would gain a price advantage over all the other bait stores on Cape Cod. Frank was willing to sell me up to $1,000 on credit and never even asked for a credit reference. He told me he runs his business on instinct; somehow I was able to gain his trust in that one phone call.

However, I would have to meet Frank's refrigerated truck at one of his existing stops. It appeared that Green's Bait shop in Quincy, Massachusetts, was his closest stop to Cape Cod—a good hour's drive from my shop. I would need to hit the road before 6:00 a.m. if I was to avoid the weekend traffic and be on time for my shipment of sea worms. I estimated I would need fresh bait shipped on Tuesday, Friday, and Sunday mornings, with an occasional second midweek shipment. Sea worms could live three to four days maximum in a refrigerator calibrated for 45 degrees. If I sold half-dead sea worms to customers, I would quickly be out of business.

Since I would be on the road at daybreak on days I went to pick up fresh bait in Quincy, I needed a trusted employee willing to show up and open the bait store at 6:00 a.m. A waitress at a local fish restaurant suggested I call her cousin Danny Herring. Was God speaking to me? Danny was fourteen years old, but his face showed he was mature well beyond his adolescent self. We hit it off right away. Danny promised I could trust him to arrive on time since his home was a short bike ride to the store. He loved the concept of the business and knew we were going to have fun together. I was twenty-three at the time but relied on Danny for advice that would prove extremely valuable as the summer season progressed.

Danny's first suggestion was that we needed music. This was the summer of the Woodstock Music Festival. Danny, who had a more eclectic understanding of the music of the '60s than I did, arrived at work one day with a powerful record player and assorted albums that we blasted away into the road and parking lot, giving the bait store, fruit stand, and sub shop the look and feel of a roadside carnival.

A long traffic light a quarter of a mile down the road stalled cars in front of my shop from 7:00 in the morning to 3:00 in the afternoon on busy summer weekends. The unexpected barrage of popular music caught travelers by surprise as they read my sign, Discount Bait Store, and waved their approval. My hope, of course, was that they might pull in to see what a discount bait store was all about.

Danny would work the early morning shift whenever I raced to Quincy to pick up fresh bait and often spend the rest of the day keeping me company and enjoying the host of characters and customers who frequented the store. I had brought to the store a small library of books on comparative religion, yoga, philosophy, mysticism, and esoteric theology—all subjects that had caught my imagination in college. My thirst for spiritual knowledge was ongoing, prompted by certain mystical experiences I had had as a child.

Danny wanted me to teach him everything I knew on all these subjects. He and his mother belonged to a Spiritualist church, and he was eager to learn more. He borrowed many books and returned them the next day, filled with questions and excited by his newfound knowledge. I loved our time together and could not believe how much we enjoyed each other. Some evenings, Danny would bring one of his many girlfriends to meet me. If it seemed like an important date for him, I would suggest he dip into the cash box and take out whatever money he needed.

On the third morning of my first week in the bait store, I arrived at 6:00 a.m. to discover that someone had unplugged the outside heavy-duty extension cords powering the three refrigerators that kept my sea worms alive. After this happened on two consecutive nights, I had my suspicions of who might be sabotaging my business. I had been experiencing hostile looks from the direction of the Bay Sub, likely due to my beard and general hippie appearance.

Betty, who owned the fledgling business, had allowed her daughter's friends, three homeless adolescent boys, to live in the back of the store. As if that weren't enough to put her at odds with the health inspector, Betty had brought a menagerie of her favorite pets to live at the restaurant. Two stray dogs, a deodorized skunk named Benjamin, and a hamster named Marty all called the Bay Sub their primary residence. Benjamin spent most of his day in a cage in the shadows of the store unless it was exercise time, when he was given free reign to wander among the chaise lounges that were scattered around in the back of the shop and served as beds for Betty's extended family. Marty the hamster burrowed a home for himself in the crate of napkins closest to the cash box and would pop out unexpectedly when Betty would make change for her few daytime customers.

Betty's face showed the strain of a hard life. She easily weighed in at over 300 pounds and would sweat profusely under the pressure of taking an order for more than one sandwich at a time. Yet she was pretty and had a kind and warm smile. I knew I had to win Betty's friendship and hope she could control the threatening behaviors I was experiencing from the boys who hung around her sandwich shop.

Once I made a plan, I closed the bait shop for half an hour to gather supplies. I purchased a cheap portable grill, charcoal, chicken, corn on the cob, potatoes, and quality paper plates. With an assortment of spices, I prepared Betty a Texas barbeque. When the dinner was complete, I arranged the meal nicely on a plate and walked over to the take-out window of the sub shop.

"Betty," I said, "I prepared you a little something since I thought you might be hungry." I removed the cover and presented the meal with the fanfare of a French chef. It looked and smelled delicious.

Betty was caught off guard and almost tearful at my gesture to do something special for her. All she could say was, "what can I do for you?"

I certainly was not interested in any food that was touched by Betty or the boys. For all I knew, Benjamin the skunk might have peed on the ten-pound baloney that never seemed to find its way back into the refrigerator. "No thanks, Betty, maybe some other time" was my constant refrain whenever she offered me a sandwich.

From that moment on, Betty and I became good friends. Not casual friends, but good friends who were always ready to help each other out. Betty's only hope of selling subs to locals or tourists was centered on her shop being open all night. After some of Betty's late-night,

semi-inebriated customers inquired whether they could buy some bait to fish an early morning tide, Betty offered to sell my bait along with her sandwiches. Although the idea of offering a late-night special of a loaded submarine sandwich and a dozen live sea worms may not sound appetizing to the average tourist, it apparently appealed to Betty's clientele. Almost every morning, when I arrived at the bait shop at 6:00 a.m., I would check in with Betty, who often greeted me with a big smile and a paper cup stuffed with bills and change.

Now that Betty and I were on friendly terms, the sub shop boys no longer saw me as an outsider; the tampering with my electrical hookup ended with the Texas barbeque. I was amazed at how a small gesture on my part could so quickly change my status with Betty and the boys.

I was beginning to discover how love and service to others was a powerful solvent for misunderstanding and oppositional behaviors. Our friendship lasted well beyond my first summer at the bait shop. Over the next few years, as Betty managed to stay one step ahead of the board of health inspector, her hand-painted plywood sign would reappear in the windows of different rundown properties along the road. Whenever I showed up, I always got a big smile and a smothering hug.

During my first week in business, a man dropped by the bait store and offered to sell me a forty-pound burlap bag full of live green crabs. Crabs are the food of choice of a fish called *tautog* or black fish. Tautog are strong, hard-fighting fish with a set of well-formed human-looking teeth. Their diet of crab makes their meat taste sweet, like lobster. My grandmother loved serving this fish to guests.

The guy wanted only ten dollars for the bag, so

I was willing to give it a try. I knew the crabs would never survive the night in the burlap bag, so I searched the woods behind the Bay Sub and found a sheet-metal trough similar in style to what bricklayers use to hand-mix concrete. I figured I could put all the crabs in the trough with a little water and cover the top with window screening.

It was a Friday night and the serious fishermen were working their way through weekend traffic to their favorite fishing spots on the Cape. It being my first Friday night in business, I didn't know what to expect. To my amazement, it turned out to be a great night and I sold almost $200 in bait and tackle. However, at fifty cents a dozen, I was only able to sell a dollar's worth of crabs. I figured I had over 500 crabs left in the trough when I tucked them in for the night and headed home.

The following morning when I arrived at 6:00 a.m. to open, my neighbor, who ran the Ace TV Repair shop adjacent to my store, met me with a shovel in his hand and a scowl on his face that made me think he was ready to rap me on the head. Evidently, my trough of crabs were able to free themselves during the night by slipping under the window screening and, seemingly preferring the soft grass of his lawn to our dirt parking area, now littered his yard—all 500 or so lying dead on their backs, claws in the air.

I promised to immediately search out and remove all the crabs from his yard. I swore I would not open my shop until he was satisfied that every last crustacean was off his property. By nine in the morning, I was able to sound the "all clear" and bury the dead crabs in a hole deep in the woods behind the Bay Sub.

One afternoon, Danny brought in a 45 record that he thought would liven things up around the bait store. The song was titled "A Simple Song of Freedom," written by Bobby Darin and performed by a well-known folk singer of the '60s named Tim Hardin. This song shared Bobby's antiwar sentiments during the late stages of the Vietnam War. The song somehow raised my spirits, since I would also face the draft once I graduated from college. The recording so inspired me that I played it continuously all day long, blasting the music into the stalled traffic backed up by the traffic light. Before long, Red became addicted to the song as well and insisted that I play it loud enough so his few customers could hear it as well.

By the middle of June, the domestic calm that permeated my living situation at my grandparents' summer home was beginning to deteriorate. The late '60s were a time of extreme polarization in America. The Vietnam War was tearing families apart, forcing unwilling young men to choose between forced enlistment, fleeing to Canada, or incarceration. The antiwar movement was strong at my university and supported by the respected professors of the political science department. Facing the draft in less than a year felt like a crushing moral dilemma.

We were far from being a military family, yet Grandpa's sentiments clearly supported the established order. He also seemed embarrassed by my facial beard and hippie appearance when guests came to visit. Grandpa was unable to see that my opposition to the war and the social injustice issues of the day came from a love and appreciation of the freedoms we so enjoy in America. I was far from anti-American; I just wanted the killing of poor people to stop, both in America and around the world.

Unfortunately, Grandpa and I were unable to keep our political beliefs to ourselves. It threatened him that I could oppose any position he took in world affairs. He was always viewed as the source of wisdom in the family. I loved my grandfather deeply and was more bothered by his sarcasm toward me than by his political views. Grandma often came to my defense. She was concerned that our political shadow boxing could permanently scar our relationship.

What helped to anchor our relationship was Grandpa's respect for my perseverance and hard work in establishing my small roadside business. I worked from 6:00 a.m. to 11:00 p.m. on weekends and twelve-hour days during the week. I took Tuesdays off only when it was not before or after a holiday weekend. Grandpa routinely asked how my sales were when I would collapse on the floor in front of the TV at the end of my work day. His sentiment toward me softened when I bought him a gift of a hand-carved whale to hang over the doorway to the living room.

My grandparents moved down to the Cape house full time around the Fourth of July. I had the house to myself except for weekends in May and June. One afternoon when I was alone at the house, sitting by the water, I noticed a woman on the beach in a pink bikini. She appeared to be collecting seashells and was bending over as if posing for the *Sports Illustrated Swimsuit Edition*.

Thinking she might be trying to attract my attention, I introduced myself by making small talk about the shells on the beach. She told me she was from Dallas, Texas, and had moved in just four houses down the beach. She had a pronounced Southern accent and could have been a character in *Cat on a Hot Tin Roof*. I told her I was Mr. Davis's grandson and about the bait store. She listened as if I were telling her the South really won the Civil War. "How wonderful," she said, "I would love to see your store."

When I asked for her name, she answered, "Nancy Rice, but some like to call me Mrs. Robinson." There wasn't a person of my generation who did not know of the role played by Anne Bancroft as Mrs. Robinson in the movie *The Graduate*. Since Grandpa would go through the roof if he knew I was involved with one of his neighbors, I decided to keep the affair off the radar. It turned out that Mrs. Robinson had been dating the owner of the Red Top Bait shop down the road from my store. He was one of the bait store owners who would not let the worm wholesaler sell to me, so I felt especially pleased to be "dating" her.

Nancy loved to come by the bait store and flutter around the customers who would appear at my drive-up window. Nancy was an eccentric personality and often arrived at the store in her bathing suit. What she lacked in intelligence, she made up for with cleavage. Nancy insisted on going along on my early morning runs to pick up fresh bait coming down from Maine. Her large, air-conditioned Ford sedan was a much better vehicle to transport live sea worms than my tiny Volkswagen.

Within a few weeks, however, Nancy began to drive me crazy. The difference in our age caused me to feel embarrassed and ashamed of my indiscretion. I was happy to be her friend since I sensed how lonely she was while her husband was working overseas. It was around this time that an elderly neighbor tipped Grandpa off as to what was going on.

One weekday night around 9:00 p.m. Nancy called me on the phone in the hope that I would pay her a little late-night visit. Grandpa answered the phone and when he asked her what she wished to talk to me about, she told him she needed my help hanging some curtains around the house. One look from Grandpa said it all. If I did not end this relationship immediately, I would find my belongings thrown into the Cape Cod Canal heading for New Bedford on the outgoing tide. Although that was the end of my affair with Mrs. Robinson, we remained good friends for many years.

I had set a schedule to pick up fresh bait in Quincy on Tuesday, Friday, and Sunday mornings. Holiday weekends might require an extra trip to Quincy midweek to ensure I would not run out of fresh bait. I learned to order my worms according to the moon's effect on Maine tides. A "long tide" would give the worm diggers extra time to work the worm flats and focus on harvesting the largest worms available. During nights of "short tides," diggers had to harvest every worm available, regardless of size, to fill their orders. I tried to avoid ordering on short tides when the worms would be of sub-par length and leave my customers dissatisfied.

The travel time to Quincy was just under an hour, but the return trip could take up to two hours if I got caught in weekend traffic. I knew that Danny was doing a good job covering for me at the store, but I still felt a deep personal need to greet all my customers. According to the arrangement with my worm wholesaler, I was to be waiting outside Green's Bait Shop between 7:00 and 8:00 in the morning. If I was late or if the truck came early, Mr. Green agreed to separate my order from his and keep it in his store until I arrived.

Green's Bait Shop was located just a few blocks from Wallace Sands Beach. The store had the pungent aroma of dead fish and stale salt water. The floor appeared not to have had a good washing since the end of the Korean War. You definitely would not adhere to the five-second rule if you dropped an Oreo cookie on the floor of Green's Bait Shop.

Mr. Green, now in his fifties, had suffered from polio as a child yet maneuvered around the store with lightning speed with the aid of leg braces and hand crutches. This was especially impressive since he was the only worker at the store and worked seven days a week from May to November. Nevertheless, I was suspicious of his offer to let me hang out at his shop and suspected he was plotting to take advantage of me. Bait store owners don't steal your cash; they steal your worms.

My concern was that if I arrived late for my pickup, Mr. Green might help himself to a few handfuls of my sea worms from each box of the ten dozen worms I ordered. I could have allayed my suspicions by recounting the worms in each box when I returned to my store, except that sea worms can get pissed off if you touch them too much and are capable of biting your fingers with their little black pinchers. Instead, I decided to arrive on the early side and hang out with Mr. Green and his customers until the worm truck pulled in on pickup days.

My customers were beginning to ask me if I carried frozen mackerel. Striped bass, Cape Cod's premiere game fish, feasted on wild herring in early spring when the herring returned from spawning in streams and rivers that flowed into the Cape Cod Canal and Buttermilk Bay. Fisherman could catch their own live herring to use as bait with handheld nets. Once the herring's run to the sea was over, around the first of June, striped bass went in search of mackerel.

While waiting for my worm delivery, I noticed that Mr. Green had a few trash barrels filled with dead mackerel, which were floating among blocks of ice and which Mr. Green was selling to his customers. With the Fourth of July weekend just a few days away, I needed to secure a supply of mackerel that I could freeze in plastic bags and sell to my customers—it was imperative that I have a full selection of bait products.

We quickly settled on a price of forty-five cents a fish, which was only slightly discounted from the price he was selling to his customers. I decided to purchase only fifty, since I had virtually no room in my Karmann Ghia for transporting anything beyond my worm order. Mr. Green packed the mackerel in empty worm-transport boxes. Each box was four inches high and thirty inches long. He was able to pack ten fish in a box, which added five more boxes to fit into my car.

Now, the mackerel is known to be the king of smelly fish. Even fresh, this fish has a distinct aroma due to its oily meat and skin. Few people are willing to cook this tasty fish in their home oven because the smell can linger for a week.

I packed as many worm boxes as possible into the tiny back seat of the car, until they totally obscured the view out the back window. The five boxes of mackerel were carefully placed on the passenger seat where I could keep a watchful eye to make sure they didn't tip over. This left me with four boxes of worms on my lap as I headed to the highway to try to beat the Saturday morning traffic to the bait store.

Once I exited the highway onto Route 28, I found myself in heavy traffic. I grew concerned that Danny would soon run out of sea worms for our customers. What's more, the heat of the day began to mount in my un-air-conditioned Karmann Ghia and the mackerel were beginning to stink. I became impatient and frustrated and started tailgating a truck in front of me, hoping it would speed up or change lanes and get out of my way. When the truck came to an abrupt stop to avoid going through a yellow light, I was forced to slam on my brakes.

My sudden stop propelled the five boxes of slimy mackerel out of their containers and onto the floor of the car. Some of the fish slid behind the gas and clutch pedals. It made no sense to pull over and repack the fish. I just drove the final eight miles to the store, sweating profusely. When I finally arrived at the bait store, I worked feverishly to get the fish from under the seats and into plastic bags for freezing. After two hours of removing fish and sopping up fish slime with paper towels, I counted forty-six mackerel. That left four stowaways hidden somewhere in my car. After another hour of searching, I found one more fish tangled in the wires under the seat. I never found the three missing fish and prayed that Mr. Green shorted me.

Over the next few days, the smell in my car grew progressively worse. It became obvious that my ability to date a woman with a functioning nose would be impossible until I was able to buy a different car. In addition to the pine tree car deodorant that hung helplessly from the windshield mirror, I tried every available cleaning agent and even spread an inch of Arm and Hammer Cleansing Powder on the carpet mats. The only remedy that helped at all was to burn patchouli incense in my ashtray. I hoped that time was on my side and that the car smell would improve in a week or two.

One afternoon, two middle-aged men came by to pay me a visit. One did the talking while the other just tried to look menacing as hell. He told me that some people down the road were very angry with me. He said I could get hurt if I did not close my business immediately. Without giving out any names, I clearly knew I was being threatened by the established bait store owners in town. Part of me was flattered that they felt threatened by me. Or maybe they were just tired of being challenged by their regular customers as to how I was able to sell sea worms at a discounted price.

I tried to stare back at them and show I was not about to be intimidated after all the hard work I put in to create my small business. I thought it best to say nothing and not antagonize the two men any more than I had to; mouthing off would have just made matters worse. I had been in business only a month, and now was in danger of being beaten up by the worm mafia.

I reassured myself that no one would risk hurting me over the sale of worms and tried to wipe the incident from my mind in the hope that it was all a bad joke. I thought of talking to my grandfather about it, but he would have blown his stack and immediately called on his friends at the state police to pay a little visit to the stores I suspected were behind this threat. I decided not to say anything that would upset my grandparents.

A week later, on my way home after closing the store, I noticed a car following me. To be sure I was not imagining anything, I took some sharp turns down side streets. The car sped up and stayed right on my tail. I did not want them to know where I lived, so I headed back to the highway. At the rotary by the Bourne Bridge I noticed a sign that read, "State Police Barracks." I made a quick turn off the rotary and drove to the front door of the police station. Once the people following me saw me get out of my car, they must have assumed I was about to report the incident and drove away. I never actually went into the building. After waiting a few minutes, I felt safe to drive home and was not followed.

I shared what had happened with Red the next day. He listened quietly then went to his truck and brought me a wooden baseball bat. He said I clearly needed it more than he did. I never discussed the danger I might have been in to anyone other than Red. He seemed to have had experience in such matters.

The loud music and sexually explicit signage ("You're in good hands with the Master Baiter"), along with my scruffy appearance and the general ambiance of a discount bait store, made my store a magnet for every eccentric and daytime bum on Cape Cod.

One regular visitor to the bait store was a retired gentleman from New Bedford, Massachusetts, named Irving. We met when I arrived one morning to find Irving picking his way through empty sea-worm boxes, hunting for dismembered or dying worms he might be able to revive long enough to thread on a hook for a morning of fishing. Irving was living on minimal Social Security benefits, which didn't allow him the luxury of paying for his bait. He wore the same old shorts with paint stains, sneakers with no laces, and a threadbare tee shirt. Irving rarely shaved and when he smiled, which was most of the time, his mouth showed just enough chewing teeth to soften the flaky white meat of flounder or cod.

Irving would stop by whenever the weather was reasonable and the tides of the canal were right for fishing. He was full of lighthearted fun and eager to share his knowledge of local fishing spots with my slow dribble of customers. Irving loved making people laugh at his bizarre antics. My favorite routine of his involved pretending he was painting the trim of my building using a mackerel as a paintbrush. Irving would delicately dip the fish's tail into an imaginary paint can. If he had been wearing a French beret and had a well-twirled mustache, you might think you were looking at Salvador Dali.

We quickly became good friends. Irving lived with his brother in a rundown house they had inherited from their mother. His car, a vintage Plymouth, had more Bondo than actual metal holding it together. With minimal income that kept him just out of poverty, Irving was able to retire into a life that seemed dignified and carefree. As long as he could keep a roof over his head, and had enough gas money for the trip to Cape Cod, Irving could join the society of fishermen. Irving showed up early in the morning to scavenge through my trash for bits of usable bait. It was my pleasure to donate a few worms that were not yet on life support. He would drop by again around two in the afternoon to show me his catch of the day. Irving preferred flounder or cod to take home for his dinner and happily gave me any pollack he caught, which I would hang off a broomstick from one of the sandwich-board road signs announcing the entrance to the bait store—proof that my bait caught real fish.

Irving was happy to watch the store for me on some afternoons, which allowed me a few minutes to cross the street to a local restaurant and grab a quick bowl of clam chowder and a chance to wash up in hot water to remove the scent of bait from my hands. Irving mixed well with the other characters who came by the store for a visit most any day.

In all our meetings together, Irving's brother remained in the passenger seat of the car, dressed in a suit and hat as if it were Sunday and he was heading for church. When I once asked about him, Irving simply told me he was fine and to ignore him because he suffered from an emotional disorder. His brother seemed perfectly happy to just sit in the car, watching the goings-on.

One Saturday afternoon, an aging black Cadillac pulled in to the parking lot. A rather short and masculine black woman, who walked as if one hip were considerably shorter than the other, stepped up to my outside service window to check out my list of bait offerings and selection of tackle. The car had six other passengers, from a grandmother to young children, but they all remained in the car with seemingly no curiosity as to what I was all about. By the look on this woman's face, I knew I was in for trouble.

We began our interaction by her wanting to see the size and vitality of the sea worms I was selling. Every worm I happily displayed was either too small or too dead for her liking. "With all due respect," I said, "we're not picking out gemstones here; these are Maine sea worms from the Sheepscot River." Her response was a disgusted look for my tone and sarcasm. She reminded me of the entitled Jewish matrons of my youth who would carry on as they directed some young deli worker to find them "a nice whitefish."

Before committing to the quantity of bait she *might* consider purchasing, she wanted to check out my selection of hooks, rigs, and lead sinkers. I knew for a fact that my prices were lower than my competitors' down the road, but, again, I got the same caustic response. We appeared to be heading for a stalemate that would leave no one better off. I had the feeling she was sizing me up as another person who was out to take advantage of her hard-earned cash.

I decided to abruptly change the combative nature of our interaction. Something in her face led me to believe she was an honest person. "I have an idea that might help us," I said. "I am going to leave my store for a while and read my book on my hammock under that tree. Why don't you come in and count out whatever worms and bait you want and select whatever tackle you need and leave your money in the cash box under the counter."

To assure her that I meant what I said, I exited the bait shop and immediately headed for my hammock without giving her a passing glance. Once I settled with book in hand, I could see out of the corner of my eye that she was busy accumulating her purchases. In about fifteen minutes, she came over to my hammock with a list drawn up on some cardboard she found in the store. This time she approached me with a handshake and introduced herself as Doris. The total was over eighteen dollars, which would have been the largest amount anyone had ever bought at one time. In addition to paying for her purchases, she insisted on giving me an additional crisp ten-dollar bill as a tip. Who gives a tip for bait?

Doris became a regular Saturday customer. She often arrived in a caravan with other cars full of families who always greeted me warmly. There was no longer a need for me to leave my shop; we had learned to trust each other the instant I gave her free run of the store. Doris was in no way the surly person she first appeared to be. She was extremely generous and loyal and the matriarch of her extended family. I often wished I had time to close the store and spend the day fishing with Doris and her family. What fun that would have been!

When business was slow or nonexistent at the fruit stand, I would hang out with Red to try to understand how he could possibly support his family selling overripe fruit and veggies by the side of the road. Red seemed to firmly believe that it was best for his business to keep the fresh produce in the back of his truck and not display it until the overripe produce sitting in the hot summer sun had sold. Thus, a case of perfectly good cherries might have to stay in the truck until they became overripe themselves. When I tried to point out the folly of this method, he quipped, "Listen, Rod, I've been selling produce since before you were born. My son manages another very popular stand back in Brockton."

The name Rod was earned shortly after I opened, when I decided to rent out fishing rods and reels for a day of family fun. I set up five rods with flounder rigs and would guide new customers to try fishing off a few bridges in Onset Harbor. Fishing from a bridge did not require the difficult skill of overhead casting.

To announce this service, I painted a thin sign that I hung over the door of my store. It read, "Rod Rental." Somehow, Red was convinced that the sign over the door was an announcement of my name and referred to me as Rod Rental. The name stuck and for as long as I operated the bait shop, everyone called me Rod Rental.

Red arrived each morning with an eclectic assortment of characters to keep him company while he ran the fruit stand. His business was never what you would call brisk. Even on the Fourth of July weekend, the cash cow of Cape Cod weekends, Red's fruit stand was pretty much a one-customer-at-a-time operation. I had learned not to bother trying to carry on intelligent conversations with Red's traveling companions. Aside from helping Red to unload produce from his truck, he never allowed them to interact with the customers. I assumed they were Red's relatives and just enjoyed an outing with him to Cape Cod. This is what made it so incredible when I met Robert for the first time.

Sunday mornings were busy at the bait store until around 10:00 a.m. By early afternoon, most weekend fishermen were heading home and business became nonexistent. I would either close up early or spend the time sitting in a lawn chair outside the store, reading from my collection of books on philosophy and Eastern religious traditions. One afternoon while reading, I noticed a man in his seventies, dressed in blue work clothes, pacing in front of where I was sitting. Assuming he had arrived with Red, I tried to ignore his presence. I was deep in thought and did not want to be sidetracked into meaningless conversation.

The book I was reading at the time was titled *Fourteen Lessons in Yogic Philosophy* by Yogi Ramacharaka. The man, whose name I was to learn was Robert, meekly approached and asked me if I knew how Eastern yogis would prove the existence of God. His question was the lead-in to what became a six-hour discussion on what theologians call "the causeless cause."

I immediately felt a connection to this man, whom I recognized as having deep spiritual insight. He talked not from intellectual theories or book learning, but from his own personal experience. He said he was once an ardent believer in Christian Science and the spiritual writings of Mary Baker Eddy and Phineas Quimby. He told me he decided at one point to test the workability of what he was studying. For example, if his car was broken down on a country road, instead of panicking or heading out for help, Robert sat patiently in prayer and calmly asked the forces that organized the universe to send him the help he needed.

Robert also had knowledge of the Gnostic literature of the early Christian church. The Gnostic gospels provided a pathway to spiritual illumination, believed to have been taught by Jesus and his disciples. Since the Gnostic gospels encouraged an individual path to God that did not require an intermediary like the Catholic Church, the followers were persecuted and the movement was forced underground. Robert told me that he was once able to study a book called *The Master Key System* by a Gnostic scholar with the last name of Haines. Robert said that the books were confiscated by the Catholic Church and that few copies remained. He recommended that I search for this book in my travels because it might open me up to information he felt I was searching for.

When I asked Robert how he had obtained his religious and spiritual knowledge, he explained that he retired from a long career as a conductor on a train that traveled between Boston and San Francisco. He told me that as a conductor, he often met people on the trains who were eager to share knowledge that was once reserved for initiates in secret societies.

The night sky glittered with stars, and neither of us could believe we had talked the day away. Red was packing up and called for Robert to get into his truck for the ride home. When I said good-bye, I told him I wished we could talk again, but somehow we both knew it would never happen. I searched for the book he had mentioned whenever I was in a city that had a large collection in its library, but was never able to find it.

Long work hours, poor diet, and a lack of sleep had begun to take a toll on my body. I felt tired most days and fought to stay awake while driving to Quincy in the morning to pick up my orders of sea worms coming down from Maine. A few times I even dozed off on the highway and began to worry about my erratic driving. To make matters worse, I was collecting speeding tickets at a rapid rate. It was no surprise when I received a call from my mother saying that a letter had arrived from the DMV announcing that my driver's license was to be suspended for a week once I put it in the mail and it arrived at the registry.

I was unprepared for this turn of events and decided to ignore the letter until I could figure out what to do. Closing the bait store in the middle of the fishing season was not an option. It was during this time that I first met a woman whom I referred to as the Witch.

I can't quite recall how or why she showed up at my store. She didn't own a car, so she must have arrived on foot. There was nothing unusual about another social oddity joining my daily list of visitors. While some visitors seemed falsely convinced that my store was just a legitimate storefront for a lucrative business in marijuana, others were purely attracted to the spirit of quirky fun and music that permeated our compound.

The Witch was attractive in an odd kind of a way. I assumed she was in her late twenties, but she said nothing to give away to her actual age. She had a well-proportioned, athletic body and dressed like a migrant farm worker from the dust bowl era. She had one striking physical feature that took some imagination to get around. When she smiled, she revealed two front upper teeth that were broken off at a forty-five-degree angle and slightly resembled the mouth of the shark in the movie *Jaws*. I found her strangely appealing. Besides, since I smelled like bait most of the time and drove a car that reeked of rotting mackerel, I knew my chances of dating a nice girl from Radcliffe College were temporarily out of the question.

After a few afternoons of hanging around the store, the Witch drew a map and invited me to her home. Her house was a tiny shack at the end of a long sandy road that was a challenge to maneuver in my VW. There was no name or number on the house, but I knew in an instant I was at my destination. All the windows of the house were soaped up from the inside, creating an opaque finish that admitted some light but made it impossible to see through. An inventive alternative to curtains, I thought.

Her daughter responded to my polite knocking on the door. She appeared to be around eleven years old and was proudly smoking marijuana from a corncob pipe. Her mother was hidden from view at the back of the tiny room behind an array of dead vacuum-tube television sets, each sporting rabbit-ear antennas. There were cats everywhere, which made it impossible to sit down.

The Witch quickly suggested that we all go for a ride to a nearby pond for a swim to cool down. It was already close to nine o'clock, which hardly seemed like the best time to take the family for a swim, but I could tell that she and her daughter must have been getting high since earlier in the day so the offer made some sense. They offered me their pipe, which I quickly refused. I was not much of a drug user and stayed away from marijuana, which made me paranoid as hell. My natural paranoia was already slipping off the charts.

Her directions to the pond were incoherent. I could hardly hear her mutterings and my car was bottoming out with every turn. Her daughter quickly fell asleep in the back of my car, and I soon realized I was desperately lost with these two lunatics in my car. What was about to happen next, I was hardly ready for. The Witch began to talk in a language I had never heard before. I thought maybe it was the language of some American Indian tribe she belonged to. Interspersed with the strange words, she began insisting that she was having a psychic vision of me on the side of the highway in a bad car accident. She pleaded with me to take her vision seriously. At first, I didn't take her vision too seriously, but I was also aware that the state of Massachusetts was attempting to get me off the road, so caution seemed logical. I thanked her for her interest in my safety and promised to drive carefully in the immediate future.

We gave up on the attempted trip to the pond and worked our way back to her house. I carried her daughter into the house and placed her on a mattress on the floor. By this time I only cared about getting home as fast as possible and forgetting the long and frustrating night.

The following morning, Danny could see I was

agitated. I shared with him the events of evening before. He listened carefully and said he knew how best to help me. Danny and his mother were members of a local Spiritualist church. He explained that different mediums from around the country came to this church to give psychic readings to people in the congregation who they intuitively felt were in need of guidance. There was a gathering that evening, and he suggested that I attend with him and his mother to see if they could pick up anything about my situation.

I agreed to meet them at their home. Danny's mother owned a small rooming house that catered to summer visitors. Their building was old, with few amenities and a partial view of Onset Bay. Before 1936, when the construction of the Bourne and Sagamore Bridges opened Cape Cod to general automobile travelers, Onset Beach had enjoyed a reputation as a moderately priced summer vacation destination. When the new highway and bridges skirted their way around the town, Onset Beach became frozen in time. It still had a small pier for fishing and a commercial dock with one sightseeing boat for trips through the canal. The end of the pier housed a snack bar that served bars of "pressed flavored popcorn." You could tell by the sign on the shack that the menu had not changed since the 1930s.

The Spiritualist Church is affiliated with the Spiritualist movement introduced in America and Britain around the 1840s. The church services contain elements of Protestantism before turning the pulpit over to a medium. The medium then selects members of the congregation to read for by contacting their departed relatives in the afterlife. Sir Arthur Conan Doyle, the creator of the Sherlock Holmes books, was an ardent supporter and lecturer for the Spiritualist movement.

We made the short walk together to the church for their evening service, which began at seven. The church building was hardly noticeable from the adjacent homes. A modest sign in gold and black letters announced that we were at the "First Parish Spiritualist Church of Onset." A chalkboard posted by the front door listed the name of the featured medium for that evening. Mediums had to be certified by the national organization before they were featured speakers or practitioners at church services. This evening's guest was a reverend from a church in Fort Lauderdale, Florida.

A small table was set up by the front door to collect an admission fee that likely was given to the evening's medium for her service to the church. The fee was fifty cents per person. The woman collecting the fees was wearing a yellow dress that might have been fashionable in the 1940s. She wore an artificial flower pinned on her dress just below her shoulder. Once I entered the sanctuary, I realized that most of the women were dressed in the same style, flower corsage and all. One could tell that someone was influencing the dress code. The men were mostly in dark sport coats and ties. I was seriously underdressed in my khaki shorts and La Costa sports shirt.

We had entered the church fifteen minutes before the regular service was to begin. I was told that a healing service was in progress. Three chairs were on the small stage. Parishioners who desired the personal attention of the healers would quietly take turns to sit in the chairs for the laying on of hands. The service was accompanied by music from an organ and full-sized harp. I learned later that the musicians were the reverends of the church, Kenneth and Gladys Custance. There were no children among the fifty or so people attending the service; Danny and I were clearly the youngest in attendance.

I took a seat at the rear of the sanctuary in case I felt a need to run out the door unnoticed. I was sitting among an extended family of American Indian worshipers who, I assumed, were from one of the Indian tribes still flourishing on Cape Cod at that time. The walls on the sides of the church were lined with glass-covered bookshelves. I was put at ease when I noticed that I owned many of these titles in my personal collection of spiritual books.

As I sat through the healing service listening to the harp and organ music, my body tension began to melt away. Gladys now took over the podium, and led us in a beautiful guided meditation. After a reading and the singing of some hymns, the service was turned over to the visiting medium from Florida.

She began her reading by selecting a woman in the front row. The medium told the woman that she had a mother or grandmother's vibration that wanted to be recognized. She said she thought her name was Mary, but everyone called her Mime. "Is that true?" asked the medium. Once the connection was established, the medium went on to share a personal message from the afterlife. The woman in the front row was tearful and most grateful.

However, before the message was completed, the medium turned her attention to me in the back row. She excused herself for being abrupt in ending her message with the women in the front row, but felt she needed to talk to me right away. Possibly she sensed that I was considering bolting out the back door? She said that she saw me in a small green sports car. She was not saying that I was going to be in a bad accident, but that I needed to be careful with my driving to avoid a disaster.

She then went on to share the details of a painful interaction I had had with my father when I announced that I was no longer interested in working for him in the family business after I graduated from college. She knew I felt deeply disloyal to my family, particularly to my mother for deciding to find my own way in life, without the support of my family.

Her description brought me to tears. I was embarrassed and grateful at the same time. She said I clearly made the correct decision for myself and that the pain of it all would subside in time. I can't give a rational explanation of how the medium was able to pick up on this turning point of my life, but her support was reassuring and the subsequent release of pent-up sadness cathartic.

I had no trouble believing what was told me that night. It was no surprise that I might have been heading for a serious car accident. The combination of physical exhaustion due to continued lack of sleep coupled with my driven and impatient personality made me a hazard on the highway. I needed to slow down and get my priorities in order. Besides, I was well overdue in sending my revoked driver's license to the registry.

The next day I dropped by to visit the Witch and tell her about my experience with the church medium. She suggested I send in my license the following day and said she was willing to become my driver until I got my license back. This was a very generous offer, since my trips to pick up bait in Quincy left so early in the morning. My friend Nancy, aka Mrs. Robinson, was also willing to lend me her Ford sedan for my trips to Quincy, since my car was too small to carry the boxes of worms and two passengers at the same time. I began to see that through my bait store, I had established real relationships with people who were true friends I could depend on.

My adventure with the bait store lasted two summers. By late summer of the second year, I was beginning to feel that this chapter of my life was coming to an end. I had managed to support myself, pay myself back for all expenses in starting the business, and tuck some money away for future investment. I never regretted the hard work and long hours. Although I still enjoyed my new friends who hung around the store, I began to miss a more normal social life.

One thing had become clear: I loved and needed to work for myself, even if that meant a lifestyle cut close to the bone. I would not find my path by following my family's path. I was going to have to find my way by doing what I enjoyed and sharing that joy with others.

My time at the bait store taught me something new almost every day. I learned that an aspect of wisdom is knowing how to act appropriately with people and to temper actions with love. If treating everyone with respect could bring joy into their lives, even in the humble act of selling bait, then I was performing a sacred act. True wisdom is learned firsthand through trial and error, success and failure. This is part of growing up. Regrettably, not all my transactions with the public worked out in my favor, yet there was something to learn in every instance.

The people I met and hung out with at the store were different from my peers from home and college buddies. They were born into a social system that provided few advantages. I doubted any of them were reminded daily, as I was, that they were heading toward a college education and a career path. My new friends were indifferent to status or personal importance. Most seemed content with their lot in life. They loved their families and were willing to put in long hours to support their loved ones. My summer friends, like Red, were real gems.

After the first summer, I returned to Boston University to finish my studies in business school. I was preparing to enter the corporate world of finance and management—big business. In classes we mulled over case studies of how large corporations maximized their profits by whatever means, even illegal ones.

While my classmates were eagerly preparing to enter this world of big business, I had been developing an opposing business model: thinking small. I had created my business without having to borrow from banks or investors. I chose a business that could get started with just personal savings and the help and goodwill of others. My belief was that I could grow a business from a small operation into a profitable business, as it expanded organically from its center core.

The bait store experience proved me right and put me on the road to developing the skills I needed to develop other small enterprises. I saw that if I could create a clear picture in my mind's eye of what I wanted, cultivate an attitude of joy and gratitude, and use my intuition, I could achieve any goal. I had developed faith in myself and faith in the process of using imagination as a creative engine to create business opportunities. All these skills would be invaluable to me when, years later, I followed my dream and opened a summer camp for children.

When I reflect on my two summers at the bait store, I realize that for me, creating and operating my business was my coming-of-age experience. Joining this strange society of shabby businesses and entrepreneurial dreamers was my journey into a strange land.

On certain days, everything went my way as if an unseen hand was readily extended. On other days, I faced devils and pranksters. When all seemed lost, a holy man, a mystic, a medium, or an insightful fourteen-year-old boy would lead me where I needed to go. In the end it was to become the foundation for all my personal and professional experiences to come. I looked forward with anticipation to how my destiny might unfold.

The Stress Retreat

I have always been a mega-worrier. I really can't help myself. If my wife is twenty minutes late arriving home from a night out with the girls, I'm in a panic. Most people do not understand what poor souls like me go through on a daily basis.

With the birth of my children, my fearfulness began to affect our marriage. My wife, who is a non-worrier and, in my opinion, totally naive to the dangers of the world, felt I needed to learn how to better handle my emotions. I was, frankly, driving her crazy.

We agreed that it would be best for all concerned if I could find a retreat center somewhere in the Northeast where I could learn some approaches to handling my stress. Some research led me to a three-day program taught at the Himalayan Institute in Honesdale, Pennsylvania. Swami Rama, a famous Himalayan yogi who founded the institute in 1971, introduced to the United States a new, holistic approach to medicine and spirituality. I was acquainted with Swami Rama's books and was excited to meet him and his staff.

This would be the first time I traveled alone since the birth of my children. With mounting apprehension, I departed early Friday morning in my brand-new Dodge Caravan minivan. Thrifty by nature, I decided to remove the back seats and use the van as a camper. I felt it would have been selfish to stay at the institute and pay a full forty-five dollars a night. I would be just as comfortable sleeping in the van at Jungle Jim's Campground, a half mile from the institute.

I arrived to register for the retreat at three in the afternoon. Nestled in the rolling hills of Pennsylvania, the institute offered a breathtaking setting. Our first class began at three-thirty with Phil Nuernberger, Ph.D. He explained how deep, rhythmic breathing could balance the opposing poles of the autonomic nervous system. With a little practice of this ancient yogic breathing technique, he said, we could learn to balance the effect of our fight or flight impulse (sympathetic system) with the impulse for rest and inhibition (parasympathetic system).

Dr. Nuernberger believed that the daily practice of rhythmic breathing was a powerful tool in mitigating the ill effects of stress. We practiced by sitting quietly and learning to breathe using our diaphragm. Each full inhale was balanced with a controlled exhale of the same duration. The practice sessions were deeply relaxing.

We broke for dinner—a wonderful variety of vegetarian dishes I had never tried before. Following dinner, we entered an auditorium to hear a talk by a woman from England who must have been in her eighties. She described her experiences as a devotee to a guru (a spiritual teacher) in India.

She explained that she had been married three times, and that each marriage had been cut short by the unexpected death of her husband. In an effort to find her way in life, she decided to go to India and seek a spiritual teacher.

The woman stated that while the rewards of spiritual development were great, the process of working closely with a guru was like being hit by a truck. She told us thrilling tales of the many personal trials her teacher put her through. On two occasions, she was put on a train headed for Calcutta with absolutely no money or resources. Her challenge was to survive in this city noted for its extensive slums and return safely to her teacher in two weeks. As I listened to her riveting tale, I felt that it might be helpful for me to be challenged in a similar way. Was the source of my stress rooted in living a life that was too ordered and secure?

I pondered this question as I returned to Jungle Jim's Campground. When I had registered earlier at the campground, the owner felt that since I was sleeping in a van, she should put me in a different section from the tent campers. She pointed out an empty field used for overflow campers on holiday weekends in the summer. She said that since it was still May, she and her husband had not yet moved to the campground to live.

She would return sometime after nine in the morning.

I rolled out my sleeping bag and prepared myself for a cold night on top of a mountain. When some small flying bugs tried to enter my van, I made sure that every window was closed tight. I usually feel safe in the woods, but for some reason that night I felt I should lock myself snugly in my van.

Around two in the morning, I awoke due to the demands of my bladder. I fumbled with the lock of the sliding door in the dark and was able to open it partially, to depart for a quick pee in the woods. My van was parked on a slight incline and after I got out, I heard the door slide closed and click shut. I shuddered with horror at the thought that I might have set the door to lock by mistake.

I ran to the van and found that the door was indeed locked. I circled the van three or four times trying each door, searching for a way back in, but with no success. I stopped to size up my situation: I was wearing only my white Jockey underpants. I had no tee shirt or even socks to protect me from the cold. My keys and wallet were, of course, in the van along with my glasses. A rush of intense fear coursed through my body. The temperature had fallen to below freezing during the night. My teeth were beginning to chatter uncontrollably.

I felt I was now in danger of hypothermia. "To hell with the stress retreat," I told myself. I needed to get into my car immediately. I began searching the field on my hands and knees for a rock to break a window to get in but found none, since the field was smooth so the grass could be easily cut. At last I was able to find three rocks around the size of a golf ball. In desperation, I started throwing the rocks with all my might at the passenger side window of my van. Here I am, at a stress retreat and on the first night I'm there, I'm throwing rocks at my new van!!

The window refused to shatter. I tried holding a rock in my hand and tried again to smash a window. After one helpless try, I stopped myself. If I was able to break the glass with the rock in my hand, chances were good that I might cut my wrist severely, which could be life threatening.

I remembered that only a few hours ago, after hearing the story from the woman from England, I had wondered if I was ready for the type of challenge she faced in India. I had to face the humor and seriousness of my situation. Had I brought this survival situation on myself without being consciously aware of it?

I remembered the breathing practice we had learned that afternoon and decided to try it. After a few controlled breaths, I began to calm down and regain some composure. Once I could think again, it made sense to head for the restrooms up the hill in the center of the campground, hoping I would not be spotted until I could hide behind a tree or shower curtain. Who knows what would happen if people saw a naked madman running around the campground in the middle of the night?

When I reached the restrooms, no one was around. I turned on the hot water in three showers to create some much-needed warmth in the room, then sat on a bench with my knees pressed against my chest to preserve what little body heat I still had. I must have sat there for an hour in the hope that someone would come in and lend me some clothes.

I stuck my head out the door, hoping someone was in the area. Then I saw a phone booth lit up by a large tree. In Maine at that time, you were able to contact an operator without depositing any money into a pay phone. Maybe Pennsylvania worked the same way? I was in luck; a dial tone appeared when I lifted the receiver. I dialed zero and told the operator that I needed the state police.

Within seconds, I had an officer at the police barracks on the phone. I was able to convince him I was not a crank caller and that I needed immediate assistance. "Please come get me at Jungle Jim's Campground," I pleaded. "Unfortunately," he responded, "I am stationed almost two hours away and no other officers are available this late at night to help you." As I was about to hang up, I got a brilliant idea, considering I was half frozen. I said, "I belong to AAA, could you call me a tow truck? They are skilled in opening locked cars; besides, their motto is 'We always come.'"

The officer agreed to call me a tow truck and promised to call me right back at the pay phone. Sure enough, a tow truck would arrive in less than two hours.

With time to kill, I resumed my fetal position on the bench in the men's shower room. Shortly, I heard the door of the women's bathroom open. I yelled for her attention and explained my desperate situation to her through the thin wall. Fortunately, she believed my story and soon returned with a pink running outfit. I was overwhelmed with gratitude. Now I felt confident that I could make it through the night.

Around 4:00 a.m., I heard a tow truck pull into the campground. I jumped into the cab of the truck and guided the driver to my van on the field. In the darkness, I hoped the driver couldn't see what I was wearing. I was not in the mood for any comments on my pink running outfit.

As if anything else could go wrong, the AAA driver was unable to break into my van, and was anxious to leave me and get home and back to bed. However, I convinced him I was hypothermic and needed to absorb the warmth in the cab of the tow truck. I refused to get out.

Now that he was stuck with me, the guy was able to remember that he knew a locksmith who might come to break into my car. He thought the locksmith lived with his mother; maybe we could look up the mother's phone number in the phone book. We drove back to the phone booth and hunted in the sand and gravel on the floor of his truck for a dime to make the call.

The mother was fairly incoherent when she answered. Thankfully, she was willing to wake up her son. He agreed, reluctantly, to come help me around

6:00 a.m. the next morning. For fifty dollars, he was able to pick the lock and get me back into my van. I thought fleetingly of the forty-five dollars I had wanted to save by sleeping in the van, and paid him. I had been up all night and had to return to the retreat for a full day of classes.

After breakfast, I called home to tell my wife about my night at the campground. She listened intently, as is her manner, and then asked if I was telling her about a nightmare I had that night. "Hell, no," I said, "This is exactly what happened to me."

Little did I know when I left for this retreat that my physical survival was to be put in jeopardy. The intensity of being locked out of my van almost naked on a very cold night was all part of my learning. The breathing techniques were powerful tools to balance my emotions and calm my mental state of mind. I was introduced to a new holistic approach that could produce immediate results. Excited with my new knowledge, I wrote up my own stress course and was able to teach it at two local hospitals for many years.

Nobody Is Perfect

During the early 1970s, the Boston area was teeming with training seminars and intensive personal-growth workshops as part of the new movement in humanistic and transpersonal psychology. I decided that my late twenties was an excellent time to avail myself of these new growth opportunities. I was by nature a fearful person with moderate anxiety and generally low self-esteem. I figured if I learned all I could while I was still young, I would become a better therapist and better person. I researched a number of programs and decided to enroll in two group experiences that were recommended by other therapists. Each program was expensive and each held in Boston-area hotels over four consecutive weekends.

By the end of the second program, I felt I had peeled away the onion skins of my thinking, judging self. My heart opened up with waves of pure joy. I prayed to God that I would never revert back to my former self.

I remained in a mild rapture for about a week. The world around me appeared almost psychedelic in light and color. My therapy sessions with clients were much deeper and more emotionally cathartic than usual. One evening, as I walked through the streets of Boston, I seemed able to make meaningful connections to people I had never met before. Strangers appeared to be attracted to my energy and wanted to talk to me. I had never experienced anything like this before.

Unfortunately, after a week or so, I began slowly sliding back into my former self. I was saddened with feelings of a lost paradise. When I called other participants in the program, their experiences seemed similar to mine. I went to one more meeting of this group, but was disappointed at its emphasis on getting us to sign up for additional workshops.

While fleeting in nature, these workshops made a profound impression on me. I now searched for other experiences that might have a more lasting effect on my psyche. A friend told me about a special Outward Bound program he had just completed. Outward Bound is a nationally recognized survival school founded by the British Royal Air Force during World War II. I learned that a program was being offered exclusively for teachers and therapists at one of their base camps on Hurricane Island in Maine.

I quickly filled out the application, borrowed some money to cover the tuition, and rushed to the mailbox to post my application, but couldn't let the envelope drop into the box. I suddenly became aware of what an enormous personal challenge this program would be for me and was concerned what I might discover about myself while under the intense stress. If I were unable to successfully complete the program, the personal shame would be unbearable. Still, I decided to do it.

My course began in mid-May. I can easily remember the overwhelming anxiety I felt when the thirty-six participants gathered on the dock of the Rockland, Maine, ferry terminal, our pickup spot for the trip to Hurricane Island. We were an eclectic group of men and women ranging in age from twenty-five to fifty-five. There were college and high school teachers, college administrators, a few psychologists, a high school football coach, and a Jesuit priest. The participants from academia were doing most of the talking and seemed confident they were going to enjoy every minute of our adventure. On the other hand, a good ten of us, including me, were scared to death and more than willing to share our many neurotic concerns with one another. I could see we were already beginning to bond and would be able to help one another through the trials of the experience.

The academics' enthusiasm sank like an anchor when the open pulling boats arrived. Somebody asked, "Where do we sleep and, more important, where is the bathroom on this thing?" One of the instructors held up a galvanized pail tethered to a six-foot rope. Of course, if that seemed too dainty, we were free to hang our asses off the side of the boat while holding on to the shrouds (ropes) that secured the main mast to the hull.

Our open pulling boats were the size and design of a small lifeboat that you might see hanging off the side of a merchant ship. We were a convoy of three boats, each with twelve participants and two instructors. The boats were twenty-eight feet long and came to a point on either end. With the positioning of the two masts, we had to make do with twenty feet of sleeping space for fourteen grown and soon-to-be very smelly sailors. Simple math made it clear that we would need to lie on our sides and spoon together in order to fit everyone on board.

Heavy oars were spread out over the rowing benches to serve as the sleeping surface for our old-style cotton sleeping bags. A black tarp was secured between the two masts and to the rails of the boat, affording us only minimal protection from the rain and wind. My anxiety over being cramped into small spaces along with a frequent need to relieve my bladder in the middle of the night made me think it best to place my sleeping bag at the front of the boat, between my new boat mates and the main mast.

When nature called, I wormed my way out of my sleeping bag to find the now highly prized pee pail. To my astonishment, when I returned, my space had disappeared under the force of the thirteen spooned, sleeping sailors. I considered my option of waking everyone up to fit me back into the group and realized that course of action would not have been easily forgiven. I resigned myself to try to get some sleep in the front of the boat, trading the luxury of sleeping on oars for the pleasure of cuddling alone in the open air around the sea anchor.

With almost no sleep, we rowed the next morning to Hurricane Island for a five-mile morning run, concluding with a thirty-foot jump off a dock into the frigid ocean water. My mental state, after an unforgettable night on board the boat, had severely lowered my confidence to complete the course. We were told that this was our day to develop group cohesion. Our challenges began when we were led to a fourteen-foot-high wall. The wooden wall was smooth on one side, but had staging on the back that allowed you to climb down to the ground. We had to find a way to get all twelve members of our group over the smooth side of the wall in ten minutes.

I surprised myself by blurting out a plan I thought would work: One person would stand on the shoulders of another person while both leaned against the wall. I believed I could climb up the side of both of them and, by standing on the shoulders of the top person, reach the top of the wall and get myself over to the other side. I would then be in a position to lean over the wall from the top and help other members over the top. The real challenge would be getting the last member over the wall. I felt a few of us could hang a tall member from the top of the wall to act as a rope. The last member on the ground could make a running start, try to reach and climb the leg of our human rope, and hold on while we pulled both of them over the wall from the top.

Since no one came up with an alternative plan, I quickly assigned a role to everyone. I had adequate upper body strength from years of weight lifting and easily made my way over the wall. Everything went fine until the last remaining person on the ground was not able to pull himself up the leg of our human rope. My plan was now in serious jeopardy. I quickly told my teammates to lower me down the wall. Since it was my plan, I felt I had to make it work. I traded places with the last person and helped him up on my shoulders and over the wall. Our tallest member was again suspended from the top of the wall. With my boat mates shouting encouragement, I was able to claw my way up his pant leg until I could safely reach for his belt and hold on while we were both lifted over the wall.

With our first group challenge completed, our instructors led us in a feedback session highlighting the group dynamics that led to completing the task successfully. My boat mates appreciated that I had stepped forward with a plan and took responsibility by being the last participant to get over the wall. Everyone was surprised by my leadership ability, since I had been so quiet and unsure of myself the preceding day on the boat. The instructor stated, "Now you all know you can trust Ron to come through for the group." With his generous comment, I felt a giant weight lifted from my body. I realized the power behind my anxiety was basic insecurity as to whether I could be a productive member of the group. From that moment on, my fearfulness and reticence disappeared, and I was ready to be fully engaged in this life-changing experience.

For twenty-eight days, we were constantly on the move. My favorite activities were the high ropes course, rock climbing off the cliffs of Acadia National Park, a four-day solo excursion that required foraging for food on an island in Penobscot Bay, running two full marathons, and learning survival skills. I found the training in sailing, navigation, and rowing to be most challenging. My mind wandered while rowing, and my oars continuously tangled with those of the rowers around me. Sailing requires a keen sense of direction and constant attention to variances in wind direction. I can get lost backing out of my driveway, so you can imagine how my boat mates felt when it was my turn to take over the helm on night sails.

What benefited me most from Outward Bound was not the physical skills or training I experienced, but how it stretched my awareness of what I felt I could now accomplish in my life. On the final full day of our expedition, we sailed and rowed all night and were dropped off at seven in the morning on the island of Vinalhaven, near Acadia National Park. We were promised a glorious party that evening to celebrate our completion of the program. A hand-drawn map was distributed to the group with instructions to arrive at a particular meeting hall by five o'clock that evening.

We were about to complete a twenty-eight-day adventure that included sailing in the hot sun by day and cold misty sea breezes at night. We were never afforded the luxury of ice, so our meals were mostly prepared from dried grains and root vegetables with only cool water to drink from island springs. Needless to say, the only topic aboard our boat on the last few days of the program was the anticipated pleasure of an ice-cold beer. As soon as we departed our pulling boat on Vinalhaven with our meager belongings, we huddled in a circle in the hope that someone in the group had defied one of the program's sacred rules and smuggled some money on the trip.

It was no surprise to any of us when one of our boat mates confessed that he was wearing a money belt with a twenty-dollar bill hidden inside. Immediately we flagged down a car and asked where the closest general store was. The driver seemed almost sad as he told us that the store was six miles down the road. "Six miles," we said to each other, "that's nothing. We just ran a twenty-six mile marathon two days ago!" With no further discussion, we set off on our quest to our holy grail, a frosty cold beer. We had all experienced new perceptions of our physical abilities and sharpened determination.

Of the many personal growth experiences I experimented with during that year, the Outward Bound experience seemed the most beneficial and long-lasting. Twenty-eight days being challenged at sea and on land was the perfect catalyst to discover the strengths and weaknesses of your personality. I was not the person to be counted on to command the boat during high seas. My personality was best suited as the jokester, storyteller, group facilitator, and cook. Come see me when you need cheering up or something hot to eat.

I learned there is no need to feel competent at everything. You just need to discover how you are best suited to contribute to any group effort. One afternoon, while rowing our way around the island of Isle au Haut, I taught my fellow rowers some funny camp songs I learned as a kid. My boat mates were amused by my silly and cheerful song leading, but one of our instructors was getting frustrated at my inability to keep my rowing in sync with the people behind and in front of me.

I was lost in my role as an entertainer while my oars were splashing away, out of rhythm with the rest of the boat. After many warnings, the instructor had had it. "Furst," he shouted out, "you can't row for shit!" You could feel the tension in the boat as everyone looked to me for a response. None came. Since I was feeling secure in the roles I was fulfilling for the group, his remarks, while true, were in no way hurtful. I thought to myself, "So you stink at rowing. You do plenty of other valuable things for this group." I responded to his remark by saying, "Well, nobody is perfect," and began laughing hysterically. With the tension averted, my boat mates became hysterical with laughter as well, and the instructor joined in, too. We all had learned a big life lesson: Nobody is perfect.

Two Men, Two Affirmations

Professor Peter Bertocci

During the second semester of my junior year in business school, I scanned the registration booklet to choose my last remaining elective course. I had not taken any classes from the philosophy department and wanted to round out my education by studying with Boston University's most celebrated professor, Dr. Peter Bertocci.

I was intrigued with a course he taught called Classical Metaphysics. My understanding of metaphysics was that it was related to parapsychology, in which I was most interested. The course was open only to seniors who were philosophy majors or graduate students in the philosophy department. I would need special permission from Dr. Bertocci to be admitted to the course.

I showed up early for the first class to ask the professor to sign the permission slip admitting me into the class. Dr. Bertocci was a short man in his late seventies with a very hoarse voice that was difficult to understand. He looked at me as if I were crazy. He said that the course was open only to advanced-level philosophy students. Without any background in philosophy, I would be unable to understand any of the class material and discussions. He then noticed from my slip that I was in the business school. He added that no students from the business school had ever passed any of his courses.

He seemed certain that his last remark would end the discussion so he could begin the class. Instead, I stood my ground and insisted that I wanted him to admit me. With an irritated look, he signed my slip and told me to sit down. He must have felt that I would be out the door before he finished going over the required reading list.

I was not used to being so bold and wondered what I was letting myself in for. The Vietnam War was going on at the time. If I was unable to pass this course, I could be drafted for failing to complete all my courses by the end of the semester. The student deferment delayed my being drafted. I would have to do whatever it took to pass this course.

By the end of the class, I was so confused that I couldn't even take notes. Everyone in the class was proficient in asking questions of Dr. Bertocci that showed off their knowledge of prominent philosophers. It was also clear that classical metaphysics had nothing to do with parapsychology. We would be studying the nature of reality as experienced by the classical Greek philosophers.

I waited for the right moment to talk to the

professor at the end of class. I admitted that he was correct in saying I would be overwhelmed by my lack of knowledge and asked him if he kept office hours to help out students like myself. He said that he did but added I would never show up. He said that he saw students at 7:30 a.m. three days a week and that in his many years of teaching, no students had ever come to see him. I said I'd be the first.

I am an early riser and arrived at school before seven. When I hunted for a place to park, I noticed that a parking meter was broken by the entrance to Dr. Bertocci's office. The meter was stuck on the two-hour mark so it would never expire. If I got to school early, I could park by this meter and save the five-dollar parking fee at the school lot. Always looking for ways to save money, I took this as a positive omen.

Dr. Bertocci was busy at work when I arrived. He must have been startled when I quietly knocked on his office door. He greeted me warmly and said that he was working on a new book he called *The Cosmological Argument Revisited*. I had never been to see a college professor during office hours and was unsure of myself. Taking out my notebook, I asked him to help me understand the ideas of his last lecture in class. For some reason, I found him easier to understand when he was speaking directly to me as I sat in front of his mahogany desk. He surprised me with his patience and appeared to be enjoying our little visit.

When our allotted time was over, I thanked him

and said I would be returning in two days. He responded with a slight lift of his brow. In fact, I returned two or three times a week throughout the semester, each time parking my car by the broken meter.

Dr. Bertocci really seemed to care that I was keeping up with the material. I realized that I had considered many of the arguments he presented in class and was capable of explaining my viewpoints, even when I disagreed with his personal ideas. He was encouraging me to develop and defend my ideas.

Dr. Bertocci referred to himself as an epistemic dualist. He believed that an infinite supreme intelligence set the universe in motion but retreated after its creation. The supreme intelligence no longer had a relationship with its finite creations. The infinite and the finite would never meet again. If species of animals went out of existence, that would be expected of finite creation. On the other hand, I was a monist and believed that the universe was created out of itself and therefore always contained its infinite qualities. I supported an Eastern religion approach that stated that all creation was evolving back to its infinite source.

I could not believe my good fortune in developing a relationship with a famous philosopher who was now mentoring me during our early morning meetings. Dr. Bertocci was eager to make sure I was always prepared. He was most helpful in guiding me on what I needed to review for the exams, almost giving away some of the test's essay questions. I was receiving some of the best grades of any of my courses. My other business courses were beginning to suffer, since I spent all my available time preparing for the metaphysics exam.

During our last class of the semester, Dr. Bertocci handed back our final exams to go over the material. I had scored an A minus. At the end of class, he asked me to stay a minute after class. He told me that he was wrong to have discouraged me from taking his class and that he had underestimated my perseverance. He then told me that I received the only A in the class, and for that I should be very proud of myself.

A year after I graduated from college, I was still living in Boston and decided that I wanted to sit in on some college classes that I was not able to previously take. I had no intention of paying for classes since my personal funds would not allow it. I looked up courses at Harvard Extension School and noticed that Dr. Bertocci was teaching a course on Abraham Maslow, one of the founders of humanistic psychology.

The course was taught in an old building in Harvard Yard. The room was a large lecture hall able to hold a few hundred students. The seating was banked, rising by row from the teacher's podium, similar to a theater. I got to the class early in the hope that no one was checking student IDs at the door and found a seat way in the back, a good climb from the podium. The class soon filled with students.

From my vantage point in the last row, Dr. Bertocci looked tiny when he arrived to teach the class. Before he said a word, I noticed that he seemed to be squinting his eyes and looking in my direction. Sure enough, he began to climb up the aisle until he came to my row of seats. Then he asked everyone to stand up so he could work his way to my seat, and greeted me with a warm handshake. He said he was very pleased that I had come to hear him talk about Maslow.

I was so touched that it was hard for me to say anything in return. The other students were now looking at me and wondering who I was that Dr. Bertocci would honor me in that way. At that time I was in therapy with a psychiatrist in an attempt to understand the origin of my feelings of low self-esteem. When I shared the experience of my trip to Harvard, the psychiatrist roared with laughter. He told me to try to always remember that moment when Dr. Bertocci climbed all those stairs to welcome me into his class.

One's personal destiny is difficult to understand. I do feel that life will offer us opportunities to advance ourselves from time to time. When your intuition tells you that you must take a risk and follow your instincts, you need to heed the call, for another opportunity may never appear.

Dr. McArthur

My father, desperate for me to commit to the family business, became convinced that something was radically wrong with my sense of reality. His personal mantra was "people are out to screw you and can rarely be trusted." He was convinced that my idealism could only lead me to depression and financial ruin. He backed up his opinion with an offer to pay for me to have a thorough psychological evaluation with a renowned clinical psychologist at Harvard University named Dr. McArthur. My father had recently hired McArthur to evaluate potential executives before hiring them, to try to offset his long history of being disappointed with his senior executives.

The challenge was intriguing. How could I pass up an opportunity to chat with a truly intelligent man? Besides, my favorite lunch-counter restaurant, Elsie's, was right around the corner in Harvard Square. Dr. McArthur's office was deep in Harvard Yard in an old Gothic administration building, up four floors with no elevator. His secretary was ancient. McArthur greeted me warmly and led me into his tiny office lined with over-packed bookshelves. He looked just as I had expected. He was perhaps in his early sixties with a graying beard and gray hair that was much longer and wavier than that of the colleagues of his day. He was dressed casually, wearing a tweed sports jacket with leather elbow patches. I liked him immediately.

At the beginning of our first session, he asked me if I had any idea of what I wanted to do with my life. I eagerly spoke of my desire to open my own style of children's summer camp and told him I wanted to find ways to integrate my deep interest in spirituality into the communal experience. He leaned toward me from his desk chair and shared that, in addition to his PhD in psychology, he also had a degree in theology.

For the next seven weeks we met for two-hour sessions as he administered a series of psychological and intelligence tests. I particularly enjoyed the Rorschach inkblot test, which gave him a window into my emotional and psychological functioning. We met on the eighth week to review the results. He began our session by pointing to a bookshelf in his office that was stacked with large, heavy volumes of textbooks. With the reserved pomposity that only a Harvard professor could possess, he shared that he had written all those volumes and was considered an authority in the world in evaluating psychological functioning. He added that I should consider anything he said with the utmost seriousness.

He told me I tested with higher intelligence than any of my father's current executives (which, in my opinion, wasn't much of a compliment). He was certain that I was grounded and realistic concerning my career hopes and had no doubt that I could someday create the career I envisioned. Without knowing it, my father gave me one of the greatest gifts I ever received in my life: the blessing of a wise man and the encouragement to follow my aspirations.

The Mysterious Passenger

〜✦〜

Dorothy and I first met when I applied for a job as a Head Start teacher for a classroom on Cape Cod. Dorothy was part of a three-person interviewing committee made up of parents from the school. I was applying for my first real job since graduating from college and had no idea what to expect.

Dorothy smiled and giggled throughout the interview, which helped me relax a bit. I found out later that I got the job through Dorothy's insistence that a male teacher was needed since sixteen of the eighteen preschoolers did not have a dad living at home.

Dorothy and I quickly became close friends. I learned about her heritage as a Native American and about her early history growing up on the Pine Ridge Indian Reservation in South Dakota. Her three-year-old son was my youngest student. He rarely took his thumb out of his mouth while he followed me around the classroom and looked confused whenever I corrected him for calling me "Daddy." I soon began to feel like part of Dorothy's family and moved with them to a town west of Boston to set up a communal living environment with five other adults.

Soon after we moved, Dorothy's life began to change rapidly. With the help of the Berrigan brothers—two Boston-based priests famous for their antiwar protests of the Vietnam War—Dorothy was nominated for and won a position as a delegate to the national convention of the Democratic Party, which eventually nominated George McGovern for president. She was beginning to appear on national television after she was voted to head the credentials committee that challenged Chicago Mayor Daley's control over the nomination process. Dorothy was now recognized as a player in Democratic politics. Her good fortune led her to apply to Harvard University. Dorothy became one of the few students ever accepted at Harvard who was allowed to skip her undergraduate studies and begin her education by entering their master's program.

When Thanksgiving arrived each year, I would return home to my family for a turkey dinner and to listen to the inane conversations of my three unmarried aunts. Dorothy and her adorable children spent their Thanksgiving holiday in Plymouth, Massachusetts, demonstrating against the deplorable conditions and inhumane treatment of America's indigenous people. Russell Means, the political and spiritual leader of the American Indian Movement, led the demonstrations.

Means had also begun his life on the Pine Ridge Reservation and was a passionate activist for the rights of Native Americans. He viewed the Plymouth Rock landing of the Pilgrims as the beginning of a state-sponsored genocide of his people.

In early November of 1972, a group of 500 activists including Means stormed and occupied the offices of the Bureau of Indian Affairs in Washington, DC. One of their goals was to uncover and remove the records of numerous broken treaties between the American government and the Native tribes. Our household watched the daily developments with trepidation as they were covered on the national media. After a week of occupation, the Nixon administration promised a review of Indian claims and concerns and the possibility of granting amnesty for the activists, and the occupation ended. Considerable damage had occurred to the building and some original documents and treaties were now missing. Amnesty never happened, and the FBI went in pursuit of the people involved.

A few days later as we were listening to music in our living room, a window slid open and in climbed a large Native American carrying a briefcase and small satchel. I had no idea what was going on and became alarmed but was immediately put at ease when Dorothy called out to our intruder and seemed to know him. I was unable to make a connection as to who this person was. He had by far the most intense presence I had ever seen. He was tall and powerful looking, wore a deerskin jacket and had two long braids, which hung down on either side of his chest. His face was furrowed like the Badlands of South Dakota. At first, I was unable to talk in his presence. If someone had told me he was the ghost of the famous Indian warrior Crazy Horse, I would have believed it.

A few minutes after this Indian warrior's arrival, Dorothy asked me if I would take him to a certain meeting spot on the Merritt Parkway in Connecticut. I didn't realize at the time that they may have discussed my involvement in this ride beforehand. My initial reaction to her request was that there was no way I could emotionally manage a three-hour road trip with this strange and powerful man in my tiny VW. I would likely explode with anxiety. Of course, I kept my thoughts to myself and agreed to go along with their plan.

We departed early the following morning. My passenger had little interest in enjoying a leisurely breakfast with me. I was unaware that I was transporting someone with whom the FBI might enjoy having a word. As my little car trudged along the highway of the Massachusetts Turnpike, my passenger chain-smoked nervously and kept peering out the window. My constant choking for air was not a sufficient signal to begin a discussion of the ill effects of smoking. When he finished the last cigarette in his pack, he crumpled the empty box of Marlboros, rolled down his window, and threw the box out onto the highway. This was more than I could handle. Didn't he watch the public service ad on television depicting a tearful Indian as he looks at the garbage floating down a mountain stream in the Rockies?

"What the hell are you doing?" I exclaimed. "Christ," I said sarcastically, "don't you know better than to litter the highway?" He looked over at me without changing the expression on his face.

"You're Jewish aren't you?" he replied. "Think of it this way, if you were trying to escape from Nazi Germany during the war, would you be concerned about littering?"

I immediately understood his reasoning. We were both silent the remainder of the trip. I pulled in and around to the back of a designated rest stop on the Merritt Parkway. My passenger quickly recognized his next ride by the subtle hand gesture of a man leaning against his car. He quickly exited my car, nodded a quick thank-you, and disappeared out of my life.

Camp Softball

Many overnight camps back in the early 1950s were organized around competitive sports. Young campers were encouraged to try out for sports teams within their age group and, within a week of practices and skills development, sent over to a neighboring camp for a day of competition. Winning was highly prized and occasioned broad smiles from the camp directors and camp community. Losing, on the other hand, was disheartening, and a pattern of losing created feelings of inadequacy and self-loathing among the campers.

At age ten, I was determined to be part of a softball team for eleven-year-olds at camp. I had never played Little League and had no established softball skills. However, I had made a good connection with Dick, the counselor who coached the team, and positioned myself to be around him whenever I could. I finally got to be on the team as an alternate player. As a nonstarting player,

I spent most of each game on the bench, which pleased me just fine; I was terrified of having someone hit a ball to me in a game that really mattered.

Our camp was only a few years old and tended to attract more young misfits than did the other camps that were in our competitive league. Our campers were more interested in sitting on our beds reading *Mad* magazine than playing serious sports. Most of us hiked up our pants much too high to look like serious athletes. Few of us saw sports as a possible career or a way out of the ghetto. We had been sent to camp mostly to free our parents during the summer to go to their local country clubs. We, in turn, just wanted a carefree summer with our bunkmates until we were older and had to get serious about college.

I clearly remember my introduction to competitive sports games. Dick piled our ragtag team into the back of the camp pickup truck, our only mode of transportation to the games, and off we sped to good old Camp Mendota, a few miles down the road. Try not to be too alarmed that we were not carefully seat-belted into place. The back of the truck smelled like sour milk, since its real purpose was to make daily runs to the local dump with each day's kitchen garbage. I have to admit, being huddled together in the open air like lambs to the slaughter was fun.

Camp Mendota was neither fancy nor exclusive. The ball field might have been a hay field just a few years earlier. Only the immediate playing area had been mowed, with high grass taking over the rest of the open space. We were led down to the field by our coach and into a rotting baseball dugout that smelled like horses had peed in it a few minutes before we arrived.

When we unloaded from the truck, our opposing team was already out on the field, warming up with batting practice and fielding drills. I wondered how they could possibly be our opponents. This was supposed to be a game for eleven-year-old players and younger. These boys were giants compared to us. Their first baseman, named Andy Finke, looked like a stand-in for Prince Fielder (currently of the Texas Rangers). Andy was strong, tall, hairy, and highly intimidating. Their other star player, we soon learned, was nicknamed "The Machine." He also looked to be fifteen or older and could cover his shortstop position like a cat. We could easily see that nothing we were capable of hitting would ever get by him. We complained to our coach that the Camp Mendota team were a bunch of cheats. As a team, we had little talent for athletics, but were highly experienced complainers.

I think our coach shared our suspicions that a serious ethics violation was happening here, but, as he said on that day, "we're here to play ball."

Both Andy Finke and The Machine batted in the middle of the batting order. Their coach, after looking us over, correctly believed that our pitcher would walk the first three batters he faced, and then Andy or The Machine would easily belt a home run for a quick four-run lead.

After about three innings, we were behind something like 26–0. Dick tried to negotiate a double header so we could start a new game that might give our players a little hope and dignity. We were not so lucky. Their true goal was to pound our little egos into the dirt.

Camp Hawthorne Collection

Camp Hawthorne

I was one of those few fortunate people who know at an early age what career path is right for them. Around the age of twelve, I had a strong sense that someday I would have a career as a summer camp director. How I managed to turn my early career impulse into a real business is a story in itself. While I could clearly see my future in my mind's eye, I had to hold the image for years, trusting that my life might unfold as I hoped.

Looking back, it now seems as if an invisible hand guided me to situations that would be needed to run my own camping business. After completing business school, I acquired a master's degree in counseling psychology, taught special education, completed an Outward Bound survival program, and learned the essentials of light construction and caretaking—all skills that would later prove essential in operating a summer camp.

When I turned thirty-eight, I knew it was time to

make my dream a reality. Camps were rarely for sale, and in the 1980s you needed a million dollars to close a sale. Fortunately, my ongoing interest in the camping business had led me to a retired camp director who was now buying and selling camp properties. We met for dinner, and after hearing of my interest in starting a camp, he offered me the use of a camp facility he had on the market for the upcoming summer. He must have felt that he had a better chance of selling the camp property if children were present when he showed the camp to prospective buyers. He said he would rent me the camp facility, including all the boats and equipment, for the unbelievable price of $2,000 for the season.

I had enough money set aside to print a small brochure and pay the rent but little money left over for promotion or advertising. I decided to send a brochure to the middle school in my town and ask that they post it on the office bulletin board where parents might see it. I figured that since I was offering a private program, my brochure would probably find its way into the school trash can, but thought it was worth a try.

To my amazement, a week later I received an envelope with three applications and a deposit in the mail. I couldn't believe my good fortune. I would have expected a call for references before a family would send three children to a new camp. When I called the family to thank them for the applications, I found out that the mother was the school secretary. She had opened the school mail and became interested in the camp. Instead of discarding the brochure, she took it home to show her family. Now I had the confidence to move ahead and $750 to invest in advertising. Before the summer season began, I was able to sign up twenty-eight campers to start my new program.

Unfortunately, the camp I was renting was sold at the end of that summer, which required that I find a new home for the camp. I now had to face the possibility of having to give up on my future plans. I shared my concern with a friend who was a camp director in the area. He told me that a camp on an adjacent lake, called Camp Hawthorne, had recently closed, and that the camp's owners might be interested in selling their business to me, but I would first need to get the family who owned the land and buildings to allow me to take over the existing twelve-year lease on the camp property.

It was much easier than I expected to win over the confidence of the Plummer family, who owned the land and buildings, and be approved to take over the lease. I might have been their only option at the time. It was a leap of faith on my part that I would be able to pay the rent on the lease and insurance on the property for a minimum of twelve years. I was also responsible for maintenance and repairs for over twenty buildings—all in disrepair.

The business, which had closed, was selling its camp equipment for $32,000, which included sailboats, canoes, a motorboat, camp beds, kitchen equipment, and dining room furniture. I had only $4,000 in savings to go toward the purchase of the equipment. It was decided that would be my first year's payment. I would have four years to get the camp up and running and pay off the balance of my note.

In addition to the note, the sizable lease, which included the property taxes on two-and-a-half miles of prime shorefront, was structured so that the rent would not be due until May of each year. Hopefully I would have enough children enrolled for the coming summer to cover all my expenses. Providence seemed to be on my side. Whatever obstacle I faced along the way, someone stepped forward to help me.

The following stories are about Camp Hawthorne. Portions of these stories have been published in the American Camping Association's *Camping Magazine*.

Back to Basics

⌐⁌

I have always enjoyed telling campfire stories at camp. It was the favorite part of my job as director of Camp Hawthorne. Memories rush to mind when I think back to those extraordinary evenings—the warm hush that surrounded the gathering, the crackling and smell of the pine wood fire, and so many dirty feet. The campers would huddle together, eager to hear their favorite story from a summer past, less enthusiastic to work their way through a new story never told before. It was as if they waited all winter to return to camp for this gathering alone, to again be together among the tall pines on the edge of Panther Pond. Our campfire site was their Stonehenge, holy ground to most of these little earthly travelers. It was my job to help produce the magic.

At the end of each camp session, on what we called Pickup Day, parents were always astonished at the difficulty their children would have separating from camp and piling into the family car for the return trip home.

Bunkmates would hug each other, sobbing as they said good-bye to new friendships woven out of the fabric of camp life. Some of these suburban parents had previously spent endless hours arranging play dates with cousins and neighbors and engineering appropriate friendships for their children. How could three weeks of living together in the rundown shanty town called Camp Hawthorne affect their children so deeply?

Some parents probed for answers from their children on the ride home. The talkative ones shared endless stories about camp life—night talks with their counselors, new friends who felt like brothers or sisters, and, especially, camp silliness. Parents who listened patiently to their children would soon uncover the truth about life at camp. It wasn't what their children *did* at camp that was most important, it was how they *felt* at camp that gave the experience its power.

Few people would disagree that we now live in a world of consumer capitalism. Our open lands and lakefronts in New England are slowly disappearing to development. Many young children are overstimulated and overscheduled. This generation, more than any other in our history, needs the calming and regenerative powers of living close to the natural rhythms and flow of nature.

Overnight camps first appeared in New England around 1900. Camps were started by a host of individuals who had prior careers as doctors, teachers, school guidance counselors, and college and high school coaches. While land was considerably less expensive back then, these pioneers in camping relied on bank mortgages, friends, and family to provide seed money for what must have felt like a risky enterprise. Most camps had rustic buildings and sports fields that had recently been cow pastures. Amenities such as tennis courts, electricity, and hot showers were nonexistent. As the camping industry grew and competition became brisk, many camps moved away from their simple roots and developed into facilities that resembled resorts.

I have always felt that the value of a camp experience lies in taking campers out of their suburban or urban comfort zones and sharing the power of living close to nature in simple surroundings.

Back in 1918, the founder of Camp Hawthorne, Major Bigelow, searched the entire state of Maine for the perfect lakeside property to begin his camping business. He came across a small farm on the edge of Panther Pond. With over two miles of shorefront and a mile of sandy beach with fields and woodlands, it was what many believed to be the most beautiful beachfront property in the state. And Camp Hawthorne was born.

An owner of the farm property, David Plummer, built the cabins and dining hall that still stand today. The cabins were simple structures perched on a knoll overlooking the lake. Amazingly, the structures, hardly more substantial than a chicken coop, had survived the harsh Maine winters.

When I took over the lease of the camp in 1988, I was concerned that the rustic look of the camp buildings might be off-putting to some parents and/or campers. What I soon discovered was that from the children's point of view, the simple, lived-in construction of the property helped them feel more invested in the camp as their summer home.

Maybe the cabins reminded the campers of an old fort or clubhouse they built themselves with friends in their hometown neighborhood. Maybe they felt they could have built their cabins themselves with some hand tools and a box of nails.

Many of the supporting beams of the cabins were signed and dated with the names of prior campers going back as far as 1919. Campers could lie on their cots, read the names, and imagine what camp was like back then. The buildings were far from perfect, but they seemed to have a soul of their own and an aura of contentment.

A camp setting should feel like a little village where everyone knows each other by name and children are free to move around the camp perimeter with only limited restrictions under the supervision of caring adults.

Our camp was a good match for the sensibilities of the children. They could secretly add their own name on the underside of a window frame and no one minded. A projectile could pierce a hole in a screen door and, with a little duct tape, could be repaired without punishment. Each day tons of sand would be transported from the beach into the bunk on dirty feet, to be recycled and swept out the door the following morning.

Evening campfires were a sacred time at camp. Our

campfire site was situated at the edge of the lake, which gave us a perfect view of the moon rising over the water. We sat on old logs surrounding the fire pit and burned pine branches we all collected from the woods. With the campfire lighting up their faces, campers eagerly waited to hear their favorite camp stories and for the camp musicians to play and lead us in familiar songs.

Once a week, each cabin group hiked to their own special fire pit carrying food and water for a meal they would prepare themselves over an open fire. Campers sought out the perfect stick to roast a hot dog or sausage. It would be easy to imagine how their ancestors would sit by a similar fire to cook and hear the oral traditions of their people.

Canoeing down a river, sailing on a windy afternoon, climbing a mountain, learning archery, and tree fort building are all camp activities that have stood the test of time and deserve to be passed on to today's youth. Living close to nature, relying on one's own imagination to entertain oneself and friends, learning to tolerate feelings of moderate anxiety from separating from home, living cooperatively with others, and developing an independent sense of oneself are experiences that strengthen the souls of our children.

Summer camp has always supported the psychological growth of children. Living simply and communally in a rustic, natural setting away from the pressures of school life and the distractions of mass media can both comfort and strengthen the foundation of children's emerging sense of self. Nature is a wonderful healer of the soul. We all need to connect to the natural world whenever possible. Nothing fancy is needed—when it comes to camp, rustic is sometimes just what our children crave.

Jason's Story

Whenever a parent called with an interest in our camp for a child diagnosed with Asperger's syndrome, I asked to meet with the family beforehand to make certain that he or she could have a successful adjustment to camp. Jason's family heard about us through a camp referral service. His mom told me that her eleven-year-old son was a musically precocious and gifted child. His father was a musician with a renowned symphony orchestra, so I assumed Jason's innate talents were encouraged or at least inherited from his dad.

I set out to meet Jason on a snowy morning with my wife, a teacher, and our two young sons; the forecasted weather had granted them a rare snow day off from school. By 10:00, however, the weather had changed, so we felt we could make the trip with little difficulty.

Jason's mother greeted us warmly when we arrived and directed us to the den to wait for Jason, but Jason didn't appear. He refused to come down from the upstairs landing and shouted for us to go away. I could see that my two children were going to enjoy this show of power, as Jason's mother tried every imaginable trick to bring him downstairs. After ten minutes of verbal combat with his mother, I thought I might be able to break the ice by sitting on the bottom stairs with his mom and looking at brightly colored pictures from our camp album that showed the camp's setting and activities that campers most enjoyed.

By a stroke of luck, we came across a picture of a rainy-day activity in which we set up the dining hall to resemble a gambling casino. The counselors man tables for blackjack, poker, and roulette. Campers get small amounts of penny candy for their winnings. "Look, Jason," his mother said, "they have gambling at Hawthorne." Like a magic word, the idea of gambling unlocked any resistance Jason was having of going to camp. "Let me look," he said as he hurtled down the stairs to see for himself. Was this true, did Hawthorne really have gambling?

I took the liberty of exaggerating the extent to which gambling was an integral part of the camp program, with the good intention of helping Jason open up to the possibility of a new adventure at sleepaway camp. My wife and I immediately realized we had to have Jason at camp. He was wholly endearing. You could not help but love this boy at first sight. My children were not quite as positive, but felt better when they realized that Jason was not of an age that would put him in either of their bunkhouses at camp.

Jason arrived at camp and had little difficulty separating from his parents. He insisted that he be allowed to wear headphones and carry his portable tape player. This was breaking camp rules, but an exception that seemed reasonable to accommodate. We later realized that Jason brought only one tape—of the musical *Carousel*—which he listened to throughout the day. He was, after all, coming to Maine for camp—the coast of Maine being the setting for the musical.

Jason adjusted so well that we decided in the first week he could remain at camp for the whole summer. In fact, Jason came to camp for the full season for the next six summers. We had to adjust his schedule for his quirky behaviors, like setting aside time to make sand castles on the beach while listening to *Carousel* on his tape player.

Jason's hygiene was not much better than a feral child's. He fought to wear a favorite red-and-blue-striped shirt each day. On laundry day I threatened to make him walk through a car wash with it on if he would not put it in his laundry bag. Meanwhile, Jason's camp cubby had many carefully folded outfits sent by his mother, as if he were heading for a golf tournament.

Jason had perfect pitch, a natural gift of many musicians. Whenever a bell went off, a horn sounded, or a telephone rang, Jason would throw up his hands and yell out what key the sound was anchored in. He assured me ten thousand times that the camp office phone was ringing squarely in B flat.

Jason could never be rushed and needed adequate warning time for any schedule change. His sense of self would become disorganized and frantic whenever we attempted to move him too quickly into a camp van for a trip to the beach or a camping or canoe trip. He would seek me out, believing that I was behind this unsettling change of events, and shout, "We are not in rockets, Ron!"

On Jason's fifth summer at camp we discovered one of his most bizarre behaviors. Jason appeared to prefer foraging for food in barrels and dumpsters than picking it up cafeteria style in our dining room. I had allowed a local company to hold a picnic and lobster bake for their employees on our ball field and insisted that they bring their own dumpster so the lobster waste would not bake in the sun and stink up the camp.

The following morning, before their dumpster got hauled away, we discovered Jason had gotten up at dawn and climbed into the dumpster to forage for leftover morsels of lobster meat. When Jason arrived at the dining room for morning announcements, it was clear that he had gotten into something very smelly indeed. Tiny pieces of decaying lobster meat hung from his face and cheeks. When I confronted him about why he thought diving in a dumpster was a normal camp activity, Jason just smiled his infectious smile and exclaimed, "How else do you expect me to get any real Maine food around here?" He was quickly forgiven and sent to the showers while I set his tee shirt on fire. I wondered if this strange behavior might have been encouraged by his constant listening to the *Carousel* music, which featured a song about a wonderful Maine clambake.

Jason gave me the pleasure one evening of making me laugh so hard I thought I would need to be taken to a hospital to catch my breath. My fit of laughter was prompted during one of our camp talent shows where campers share their most extraordinary talents. Yes, there was the occasional piano or flute recital, but more often it was a chance to take the stage and show how you can take a piece of spaghetti and stick it up you nose and then have it exit your mouth—always a camp crowd pleaser.

To everyone's surprise, Jason took the stage and told us he was going to act out a complete episode of *The Simpsons*—a popular TV show—playing every character and even making the sounds of the opening music. By now our camp community was so in love with this camper that his antics delighted us all. No one was laughing at Jason, everyone was laughing with him. He jumped all over the stage, assuming the characters in rapid succession. The lodge roared with delight at his expressiveness and humor.

Our camp community cherished the atypical campers who were attracted to our summer programs. Many of these children were poorly equipped to create personal best friends at school or home, but at camp, with the structure and routine of camp life, they could feel part of a ready-made group of peers. These campers had a particular charm about them because they were so real. They lacked the pretense, bragging, or competitive angst you often see in early adolescent children. Their blunt honesty about their needs and feelings helped us make Camp Hawthorne a place where all campers felt free to be themselves. These individuals still hold a place deep in my heart and in my camp memories. I miss them terribly even now, years after they moved on.

The Guardian Angel

My life's work as a camp director ended abruptly when I received word that our lease on the camp property was not going to be renewed. This news was completely unexpected. I now faced the awesome task of selling off all the camp equipment and cleaning out the buildings for the new tenant. I was feeling as low as I had ever felt in my life. All the work and improvements that were done around camp over the past twenty-four summers were hard-fought. Every chair and bench I made for the camp in my wood shop over the many winters was full of memories. I raised my children as well as hundreds of other children at the camp, and all were dear to my wife and me. The burden of now having to sell everything off and take tons of old equipment to the dump was more than I could bear.

A friend suggested that I contact other camp directors in Maine, to let them know what was for sale or for the taking. Within minutes of sending out emails, my two phones started ringing off the hook. I must have talked to twenty camp owners in the first hour, all sharing their condolences but also eager to see what I had for sale. I decided to meet with everyone at my camp over the next week. They each agreed to arrive with a truck or trailer to remove whatever they wanted to purchase.

It was on that day that I first talked to Dennis, who was from a small Christian camp near midcoast Maine. Dennis wanted to meet me at my camp the following morning. The prices I was asking didn't seem to matter to him at all. I had fifty bunk beds that cost me over $500 each and were only a few years old. I was asking $140 apiece, which, I felt, was a fair price. Dennis said he was coming with a check and that he wanted all he could get into his truck and trailer. He sounded different from the other camp people I had talked to that morning. He said he looked forward to our meeting the following day.

Dennis called me twice early the next morning to assure me he would arrive on time. He was a slender sixty-five-year-old man and appeared to be in excellent health and very capable of carrying the heavy bed frames up the hill from the children's cabins to his truck. He could see I was in considerable pain, both physically and emotionally, as I struggled to help with the beds. After a few trips, we stopped by the lake under a large pine tree for me to catch my breath. It was then that Dennis gently inquired about what had happened with my camp.

I felt a deep sense of peace and love coming from this man I had only known for a few minutes. In an attempt to share my story with Dennis, I fell into uncontrollable sobbing. Dennis put his arm around my shoulders and repeated that it would all be okay and that I was a good man. He sat with me for over an hour, absorbing my deep catharsis of emotion. As the day continued, we would move a few more beds up the hill for twenty minutes or so and then sit on the ground to talk about our lives, as honestly and deeply as I had ever talked to anyone before.

I assumed Dennis was a camp owner or director or at least a camp caretaker. He said he was only a volunteer trying to help out the camp. He began to share a little about his life. Dennis grew up dirt poor in the backwoods of Maine with two unemployed parents and four sisters. He said the house had little heat and no insulation. Each morning it was his job to carry water from an outside hand pump and heat it over the wood stove so that his sisters could each take turns with the same bath water to get clean for school. Dennis stated he had little interest in being the fifth person to bathe in the same bath water. All he could remember eating on any day of his youth was potatoes with mustard. Growing up, he never even saw money and felt his parents had no income and lived on what they could grow in their garden and help from their church and town charities.

After high school, Dennis enlisted in the Air Force and was amazed that he would receive a salary of seventeen dollars a week. "What would I ever do with all this money?" he said. Dennis had never had any money and had little use for it. He later married a social worker and adopted two special needs children. Now he was retired from the Air Force and felt compelled to give most of the money away he received each month from his retirement. Dennis said, "Why would I need money when if I need anything, someone is always eager to give it to me?"

We talked more than we worked that day. When all the beds he could transport were loaded onto his truck and trailer, we added up the total to be over $3,000. I had also given him free mattresses for all the beds. Dennis handed me a check. When I examined it, I saw it was a personal check. I asked him why the check was not from the camp he was buying them for. He laughed and said he was buying them with his own money for the camp because they needed them. "Dennis," I explained, "I can't let you do this. I have money saved for myself and family, you have nothing, so how can I let you pay for them?"

His deep and natural sense of giving was uprooting all my ideas of saving money for security, emotional safety, and status. I told him he was ruining my life with his example of giving away all that he had. I fought with him for most of an hour to just take the beds as a gift from me, but he would have none of it. In our financial stalemate, he finally agreed that he would purchase them at half the price I was asking, so that I could feel I was contributing too. Dennis just looked at me and smiled. "Ron, you're a good man," he repeated with a wave of his hand as he drove out of camp.

Once his truck had disappeared down the camp road, I called my wife at work and told her that I had just met Clarence, the guardian angel from the Christmas movie *It's a Wonderful Life*. I have never forgotten what Dennis taught me by the example of his life. I did some research and found out that it was true that Dennis would give away most of the money he received from his retirement each month and that everyone in town and at the camp loved to give back to him as well. Dennis truly found a holy balance of how to live gracefully in our material world. I think of him often.

Made in the USA
Middletown, DE
10 November 2015